AIRBNB BOOM

*How to capitalize off the AirBnb Boom, Using
Rental Arbitrage, A Guide to Being a Superhost
and How to Optimize Your Listing as a Means
of Building up your Real Estate Profile*

GW00480757

Baxter Simon

Table of Contents

Introduction

Nowadays, it's becoming extremely difficult to make your money grow and achieve your long-term financial goals. The cost of living is ever-increasing, especially if you live in a major city, but it can take years before you get promoted or receive a raise at work, if these are even a possibility. For a lot of professionals, finding a lucrative side gig to bring in additional income on top of their regular salary is a must. In fact, about 64% of millennials, 58% of Gen Xers, and 44% of Baby Boomers in the United States have or have had supplementary jobs according to a SunTrust survey. In total, 54% of respondents have or have had supplementary jobs, with some of them having multiple gigs on the side at the same time (Locke, 2019).

Finding an active source of income seems to be the answer for a lot of people. However, it becomes challenging to juggle two or more gigs at once if you already have a demanding job. You might have already tried and failed to sustain multiple gigs at the same time. You may have experienced working yourself to the point of physical and mental exhaustion just to earn a level of income that helps you achieve your financial goals.

But what if there's another way? You can create a substantial source of income through passive means, like renting out your property through Airbnb.

Airbnb is one of the hottest ways to make money with your own property. Millions of people have already made a living through this platform. However, it is only possible to earn profits through Airbnb if—and this is a big IF—you know how to do it right. There are a lot of variables that you need to keep in mind and small details that you have to smooth out before you post your listing and open your home to guests.

The problem is not a lot of people know how to transform their properties into an effective and profitable business. They think they'll attract guests with a simple listing. They have no idea of what it means to be a host. Because you're reading this book, I would assume that you're also at a loss. You're probably stressing out about where to start or how to manage this opportunity as efficiently as you can.

Well, this book is here to help you. *Airbnb Boom: How to Capitalize off of the Airbnb Boom, Using Rental Arbitrage, A Guide to Being a Superhost and How to Optimize Your Listing as a Means of Building Up Your Real Estate Profile* is your guide, and it will walk you through the whole process. It contains a set of tips, tricks, and techniques that will help you increase your chances of success as an Airbnb host. Throughout this book, you will learn how to prepare your property, create and optimize your listing, become a superhost, and automate the process so you can successfully host from other cities. In addition, you will learn about scaling and buying more properties as well as profiting off of rental arbitrage if you don't have your own property.

At the end of this book, you will have learned all the information that you need so you can enter this space with adequate knowledge and confidence to achieve the best results possible. If you correctly and precisely implement your learnings from this book, you will yield incredible profits.

Without a doubt, with each day you're passing up the opportunity to become an Airbnb host, you are missing out on an extraordinary earning potential. So let this book show you the way. With or without your own property, this book can turn you into a successful Airbnb host.

Chapter 1: The Incredible Potential of Airbnb

Airbnb is a website and an app that allows people to rent properties for a short period of time. Users can look for a property on a given location based on the number of guests, beds, bedrooms, and bathrooms; available amenities and facilities; and their budget, arrival date, and departure date. They can further narrow down the search based on the type of listing (entire place, private room, hotel room, and shared room) and property (house, apartment, bed and breakfast, hostel, hotel, resort, etcetera) that they prefer.

Airbnb also allows users to search for experiences, adventures, and restaurants around their destination. Recently, the company introduced animal tourism on their website and app so that tourists can interact, observe, care for, and play with different wildlife and domesticated animals. With these features, users can find everything they need to plan a fun and exciting trip through Airbnb.

In this chapter, you will learn about the history of Airbnb, its perks, and the action plan of successful hosts.

The History of Airbnb

Airbnb co-founders Brian Chesky and Joe Gebbia met at the Rhode Island School of Design. In 2007, the two designers were living in a loft in San Francisco, and they were struggling to pay the rent. Gebbia was unemployed and almost broke. That's when he had the brilliant idea of opening their loft to guests. A big design conference was happening in the area, and he knew that hotels would be fully booked so attendees would be looking for other accommodations. He wrote an email to Chesky saying:

> brian
>
> I thought of a way to make a few bucks - turning our place into "designers bed and breakfast" - offering young designers who come into town a place to crash during the 4 day event, complete with wireless internet, a small desk space, sleeping mat, and breakfast each morning. Ha!
>
> joe

So they created a basic website called airbedandbreakfast.com, bought three air beds for $20 each, made ham and Swiss cheese omelets every morning, and took their guests around the city. After their guests had left, they realized that they had created something amazing. So they called Nate Blecharczyk, Gebbia's old roommate, who became Airbnb's third and engineering co-founder (Gebbia, 2016; Aydin, 2019).

In March 2008, Airbed & Breakfast was launched during the SXSW Festival, but they only made two bookings. Five months later, the website was launched for the Democratic National Convention in Denver, and they made a total of 80 bookings. Then, a year after they officially started Airbed & Breakfast, they changed their name to Airbnb. The iPhone app was launched in November 2010 (Airbnb Newsroom, n.d.).

Today, there are more than seven million Airbnb listings internationally. You can find an Airbnb in 100,000 cities spanning 191 countries and regions worldwide. In the United States alone, you will find about 600,000 Airbnb listings in different cities. There are more than two million people staying in an Airbnb every night on average, with half a billion overall Airbnb guest arrivals. The company also has offices in 34 cities around the world (Rapaport, 2018; Airbnb Newsroom, n.d.).

Gebbia's simple idea of welcoming guests to "make a few bucks" is now a company that is valued at $31 billion. In 2020, 12 years after they launched Airbed & Breakfast, the company is planning to go public (Tweedle & Holmes, 2019).

The Perks of Airbnb

When you become an Airbnb host, you will not just increase your earning potential but you will also reap social and personal perks from this experience. In this section of the chapter, you will see how becoming an Airbnb host will change your life for the better. For those of you who are interested in earning more income but are not too sure about the overall rewards of Airbnb, this section might just convince you to finally open your door to guests as a host.

Financial Perks of Airbnb

On average, an Airbnb host can earn up to $924 per month (Leonhardt, 2019). This means you can earn up to $11,088 a year! However, your actual earnings will still depend on a wide range of factors. There are eight common factors that determine an Airbnb host's actual earnings:

1. **Location.** The first variable that influences a host's actual earnings is the location of their property. If your property is in a remote location that doesn't get a lot of visitors, then you will not earn as much as someone whose property is in a tourist destination. It's a simple

economic law. When the demand for a service is high, the equilibrium price will also be high. In other words, you can increase your listing price if you live in an area where there is a lot of demand for Airbnbs.

Proximity to restaurants, shops, and other establishments as well as airports, train stations, and public transportation hubs are also good location identifiers. Guests are always looking for more accessible properties.

2. **Capacity.** How many people can comfortably stay in your property? How many beds, bedrooms, and bathrooms do you have? Obviously, the more guests you can accommodate in one reservation, the bigger your earnings will be.

   To illustrate, let's say two hosts have properties by the beach in Florida. One of them has a two-bedroom condo unit while the other has a studio apartment. The former can charge more because they will likely be hosting groups instead of individuals. If the first host charges $150 per night for a maximum of four guests and the second host charges $80 per night for a maximum of two guests, then each guest will have to pay $37.50 per night for the first property and $40 per night for the second property.

   This is also a basic real estate principle. The bigger the square footage, the higher the price is.

3. **Listing type.** Depending on your location, there will be listing types that guests will prefer more. For example, if there are a lot of backpackers visiting your area, they

will be looking for private or shared rooms instead of an entire place to rent. If you are located in an urban area like New York City, guests may be looking to rent a studio or one-bedroom apartment (instead of places with multiple bedrooms) for short-term trips. If your area is known as a family-friendly destination, bigger houses will be more in demand to accommodate larger groups.

4. **Amenities.** To be a successful Airbnb host, you should at least have the basic amenities that guests will need, like a kitchen, a TV, and an Internet connection. If you have additional amenities like a gym, a pool, and a laundry area in your building or property, you can further increase your listing price.

5. **Decor.** You want to give your guests the best experience while staying at your place. As much as possible, your property must feel like their home away from home, if not better. If you take the time to design the space, you can make it look cozy and inviting.

   Plus, you will also get more bookings if your place looks good in pictures. Aside from the initial impression when guests see your listing, being "Instagrammable" is a deciding factor among Airbnb users nowadays. The more attractive the interior design is, the more attractive your property is to potential guests.

6. **Seasons.** Seasons (also weather and climate) can affect your actual monthly earnings. For instance, if your property is located by the beach, then you might not get as many bookings during the rainy months. If a huge

storm is bound your way, then guests may cancel their reservations and request refunds.

7. **Price.** You will learn about pricing in more detail later on. But for now, here's an overview of how you can set a reasonable listing price:

   a. First, take into account the common variables that guests are looking for an Airbnb. These include but are not limited to your property's location, capacity, amenities, interior design, and the demand for Airbnbs in your area. Set an initial rate that you want to charge your guests based on these variables.

   b. Then, look into how much other Airbnbs with the same characteristics in your area are charging per night. You can find this information by doing a quick search on the website. Use filters to find similar properties in your area. This allows you to choose a competitive listing price.

   c. Lastly, perform a simple survey to get an idea of potential guests' willingness to pay. You can show your property to friends, family, colleagues, and other peers and then ask them to give you a price that they would feel comfortable to pay per night given the characteristics it has.

   d. Adjust the intial price point that you had set earlier based on competing prices and potential customers' willingness to pay. This ensures that you have a competitive rate.

8. **Reviews.** Reviews can make or break you as an Airbnb host. Potential guests will rely on the experience of your previous guests to determine if your property is as good as it says on the label. Therefore, you can't post a listing that misleads your guests or say that your property has certain amenities when it doesn't.

   Aside from the quality of your property, they will also judge you as a host. No matter how pretty the pictures are on your listing or how many amenities your property has, if guests don't have a good experience with you as the host, they will be inclined to post a bad review that will negatively impact future bookings.

In <u>Chapter 3</u>, you will learn how to set a rate that is both competitive and profitable so you can fully enjoy Airbnb's financial perks. When you start earning through Airbnb, there are a lot of things that you can do with that money so you can make progress towards achieving your financial goals, including the following:

- **Pay your rent or mortgage.** Say your monthly rent is $1,500. If you are completely booked for the month, you only need to charge $50 per night to completely pay it off. If you are charging more, say $80 a night, you only need to book 20 nights out of the month to be able to completely pay off your rent through Airbnb.

- **Save or invest.** Let's use the previous example to create another scenario. You can earn $2,400 if you are charging $80 a night and are completely booked for the month. That's $900 more than your rent, which will be equal to $10,800 in profits per year! You can save this amount or put it towards investments that will help you achieve long-term financial goals.

- **Acquire more property.** If your monthly earnings are enough to afford a second property in your area, you can grow your business through rental arbitrage. You'll learn more about this concept in Chapter 7.

Social Perks of Airbnb

During Joe Gebbia's (2016) TedTalk in Vancouver, the Airbnb co-founder recalled how rewarding his and Brian Chesky's first hosting experience was. He said, "Did we just discover it was possible to make friends while also making rent?"

Even if there are, though rare, cases of bad renters and hosting experiences, Airbnb still has great social benefits. You're in a unique position to meet people from your city, state, or country. You can even meet people from other parts of the world! Plus, there's always the possibility of making new friends with everyone you welcome into your home.

You will realize that most guests appreciate a host who is genuinely interested in having a conversation with them. They are excited to talk about themselves and where they come from. So if the opportunity presents itself, take the time to get to know your guests. You can really make genuine connections with strangers, improve your guests's stay at your Airbnb, and learn about places that you may not have visited before during these conversations.

In addition, you can learn from Gebbia and Chesky's first hosting experience and give your guests a tour. You can take them to your favorite spots if you have the chance. Aside from making their stay more enjoyable, you'll realize that it's also a lot of fun to be able to share these experiences with others.

If your schedules don't fit, you can give them a list of suggestions on where to eat and what places to visit. Here's a cooler idea: Print out a simple guide or map that you can give out to guests. Your familiarity with the place allows them to have a more authentic experience, and they will surely appreciate your local's point of view.

To show you just how socially rewarding hosting can be, here's a quick story:

A friend of mine who has an Airbnb in Washington DC once hosted a couple from Australia who were attending a relative's wedding. They booked the spare bedroom in her Georgetown apartment for four nights.

One day before they checked out, my friend took them to the most iconic spots in Washington DC, including the White House, Capitol, Lincoln Memorial, Washington Monument, and Smithsonian. She also took them to some of the cooler spots in town including the Blind Whino (an abandoned church that has been turned into an art gallery and workshop) and The Gibson (a speakeasy serving Prohibition-era cocktails).

In such a short period of time, she was able to start a lifelong friendship with this Australian couple. In fact, less than a year later, they were engaged, and they invited my friend to attend their wedding in Melbourne. She arrived in Australia a few days before the ceremony, and they took some time to introduce her to their friends and to show her around their favorite spots in Melbourne! Imagine the kind of connection that they were able to make for them to invite her to the most special day of their lives and, on top of that, to give her a tour of the city just days before their wedding!

As an Airbnb host, you will surely have experiences like this with people from all over the world. Sure, there are guests who would rather keep to themselves. You'll meet these kinds of people, too. However, when you find folks who are as open to new friendships as you are, you can really start something wonderful.

Personal Perks of Airbnb

The last notable benefit of Airbnb is that it helps you grow as a person. Airbnb makes it easy for you to enter into the hospitality industry from which you can learn new things. It also allows you to improve skills that you already have. Most, if not all, Airbnb hosts enjoy five personal perks from this experience. Like them, you will be able to:

- improve your interpersonal skills,

- better manage your finances,

- sharpen your creativity when marketing your property,

- build your own brand, and

- develop entrepreneurial skills.

These are all great benefits that you can use for life. But I personally think that the last perk is the most helpful of all. You can apply the entrepreneurial skills that you develop from hosting in other industries and business opportunities. This domino effect will open more doors for you and enable you to achieve financial stability in the long run.

The Action Plan of Successful Airbnb Hosts

Before you open your home to guests, you need to establish an action plan for five important reasons:

1. **An action plan helps establish goals.** When you create an action plan, you need to identify short and long-term goals that you want to achieve as an Airbnb host. The short-term goals will focus on each booking, e.g. what kind of experience you want each of your guests to have during their stay, how many bookings you want to get per month, et cetera.

   Meanwhile, since most of you who are reading this book want to become Airbnb hosts to earn additional income, your long-term goals will likely focus on your financial status and how Airbnb can help you achieve stability. However, if you want to turn Airbnb hosting into a permanent business, then you should also create long-term goals for this objective, like possibly acquiring more properties after a few years.

2. **An action plan helps you stay focused.** Remember that no one is able to achieve their goals overnight. However, when you have a clear idea of what you want to accomplish, you are able to:

   ○ make decisions that help you realize your goals,

   ○ identify what actions lead to success and what do not,

   ○ prioritize actions that actually lead to growth,

O make adjustments when necessary, and

O aim for objectives instead of instant gratification.

Your action plan will be your map towards success. It shows you the quickest way to achieve your goals so you can focus on completing tasks that take you one step closer each time.

3. **An action plan helps you manage time.** When creating an action plan, you should set one, five, and ten-year goals so you can better allocate time and effort on specific tasks. There must be a clear completion date for each task so you know how long it will take to accomplish your goals. This exercise also allows you to have realistic expectations. If needed, you can change your priorities so that you can work towards your overall objective.

4. **An action plan helps you create accountability.** When you're running your own business, it's sometimes hard to keep yourself accountable, even if the success of your venture solely depends on you. It's easier to procrastinate and feel unmotivated. But with a straightforward action plan, you will feel more accountable for your actions. You have no reason to put off work because you know exactly what you need to do and when you need to do it. You will also feel more motivated to work towards accomplishing your goals because you can see your progress based on your action plan.

5. **An action plan helps you measure success.** Speaking of progress, your action plan will also be an

evaluation tool that helps you quantify the growth of your business. You can see how many tasks and goals you have completed and whether you accomplished them on time. For each step you take towards the completion of an objective, you can see how long it will still take before you finally cross it off the board. If you notice that you haven't been as successful as you thought you would be at a certain point in time, you can identify areas for improvement and make certain changes to your action plan if need be.

Now that you know all of these benefits, it's time to learn how to create a successful action plan. A successful action plan has three parts: a check-in checklist, a contingency plan, and a growth plan.

Check-in Checklist

Your check-in checklist will contain all of the things that you need to fix, prepare, and purchase before new guests arrive. It ensures that your property is in the right shape to welcome every person who books your Airbnb. It also guarantees that you've done what you can to give your guests the best experience they can possibly have while staying at your place.

Each host's check-in checklist will look different given the property's amenities and other factors. However, these are 10 things that you must include in it:

- Clean the property and perform necessary housekeeping practices.

- Empty out the garbage and recycling bins.

- Change the towels and sheets and provide extra sets just in case your guests need them.

- Provide basic toiletries like soap, shampoo, toothpaste, and toilet paper

- Provide coffee, tea, and a few snacks to make your guests feel more welcome.

- Provide basic housekeeping items like dishwashing liquid, broom, dust pan, and extra garbage bags.

- Provide a key or other methods of door access.

- Make sure that safety features (like smoke detectors and fire extinguishers) are working properly.

- If you're renting out a spare bedroom in your home, make sure that your personal belongings are kept away and secure.

- Print a map of the city or a handy guide for tourists.

Contingency Plan

A contingency plan takes into account possible circumstances that may happen in the future. It helps you avoid any surprises that may hurt your business and allows you to prepare before disaster strikes. In general, a contingency plan will:

- protect your property, brand, and reputation as a host;

- minimize customer inconvenience and prevent negative reviews; and

- create systems that will solve problems when they arise.

Here are three steps to create a contingency plan:

1. **Identify risky events.** Create a list of possible events that could impede operations. These may include natural disasters like storms, floods, and earthquakes; personal emergencies like work-related events, sickness, and death in the family; and guest-related issues like miscommunication, damage to property, and theft.

2. **Estimate the risk of each event.** Rate each event's likelihood of occurrence on a scale from one (least likely) to 10 (most likely). If possible, you should also rate each event's probable impact on a scale of one (least damaging) to 10 (most damaging).

   Some events (like storms and damage to property) are unpredictable and may have different impact scores given certain circumstances. For these events, you should use your best guess or use statistics to estimate probable impact.

   Lastly, multiply each event's likelihood score with its impact score to see which are inimical to your business. The total score gives you an idea of how much preparation you need to do for each event.

   See table below for an example:

   For those of you listening to the audio version of this book, the attached PDF will be made available for free if you've bought the audiobook.

Events	Likelihood Score	Impact Score	Total Score
Fires	2	8	16
Storms	6	6	36
Work-related events	5	5	25

3. **Prepare a solution for each event.** After identifying risks and how detrimental they are to your business processes, you should come up with systems that will solve or, better yet, prevent them from happening. Let's use the previous table for an example.

Fires are not likely to happen given safety systems that are already in place, like smoke detectors and fire extinguishers, but they will have damaging effects to your property if they do happen. To protect yourself from possible damages, you should invest in a fire insurance policy.

Based on their likelihood score, try to assess how often it is that storms will happen in your area. They have quite the impact when they happen. Guests may cancel when there's a storm warning and get a refund, which will be taken out of your payout (Airbnb Help Center, n.d.a). Here's a solution: Unless the storm is expected to cause significant damage due to high winds and large hail, you can create a "Rainy Day Guide" for your guests that includes cozy spots around town where they can grab a cup of coffee and hangout. You can also make your place extra cozy with candles, warm blankets, and board games so your guests can still come for a staycation.

Lastly, if you think your work is going to take a lot of your time, you can still host from afar by curating a welcome basket or printing out a guide to your favorite spots around town. The welcome basket can include snacks, water bottles, coffee or tea, and bathroom essentials. Even if you will not be able to socialize with your guests, these simple touches show that you are helpful, hospitable, and amicable.

This is just an example of how you can create a contingency plan that protects you from risks. Like the check-in checklist, this part of the action plan will vary from host to host. It is up to you to assess risks and come up with solutions that are tailored just for you.

Growth Plan

A growth plan is your blueprint for success. This is where you identify goals and come up with strategies that help you achieve them. There are five steps in creating an effective growth plan:

1. **Identify business goals.** What do you hope to achieve in one, five, and ten years? Be as specific as possible.

2. **Perform a SWOT analysis.** A SWOT analysis allows you to identify your strengths (S), weaknesses (W), opportunities (O), and threats (T). This framework

gives you an idea of which areas to utilize, improve, take advantage of, and prepare for.

3. **Perform a competitive analysis.** What are other Airbnb hosts in your area offering to guests? How can you gain competitive advantage? How can you elevate your business and differentiate yourself as a host from your main competitors?

4. **Create action strategies.** Given your strengths, weaknesses, opportunities, and threats, as well as taking into consideration your main competitors and what they bring into the market, what actions do you need to take in order to achieve your business goals? What hurdles do you need to overcome? During this step, you need to come up with specific actions that lead to your desired outcome.

5. **Analyze and adjust.** You need to regularly analyze your business status so you can identify which strategies are successful and which need improvement. As your business grows, you'll learn how to set more realistic objectives and to make adjustments that benefit your business in the long run.

Chapter 2: How to Prepare Your Property

To become an Airbnb host, all you have to do is to follow these three easy steps:

1. **Create your listing.** Joining Airbnb as a host is 100% free. However, there is a 3% Airbnb service fee for hosts for every reservation. This allows Airbnb to continue operating.

2. **Decide on the parameters.** How often are you planning to accept guests? How much is your place worth? (We'll talk about pricing in more detail later on.) Do you have any rules for guests (e.g., no pets allowed, no smoking, etcetera)? These parameters are totally up to you. However, try not to set too many restrictions or potential guests may be turned off.

3. **Accept reservations.** Once your listing is live on Airbnb, users can start to book your place (Airbnb, n.d.a).

While joining Airbnb as a host is fast, easy, and free, you still need to prepare your property before you post your listing. This is true of any business endeavor—you need to make sure you're ready so you can guarantee customer satisfaction and increase your chances of success.

Having said this, we will talk about an effective pre-opening strategy in this chapter which you can implement before posting your listing on Airbnb.

Target Market

According to Kenton (2019a), target market is defined as:

> a group of potential customers to whom a company wants to sell its products and services. This group also includes specific customers to whom a company directs its marketing efforts. A target market is one part of the total market for a good or service.

Your target market will share some characteristics, including the following:

1. **Geography.** In other industries, geography means that your target market will be concentrated in the same location. However, in the hospitality industry, your target market will come from all over the map. They are potential customers who are interested in traveling to your area.

   Let's look at California as an example. Most people traveling to Anaheim are going to Disneyland, while most tourists traveling to Los Angeles want to see Hollywood. In northern California, we have San Francisco, which is known for its great art scene, vineyards, and Silicon Valley.

   These different cities in the same state welcome different types of tourists. If you're located in Anaheim, your target market is families with young kids or big groups of friends. In Los Angeles, tourists are more diverse but there's a theme they're all interested in— film, TV, and the actors starring in them. In San

Francisco, you have artists, art enthusiasts, techies, businesspeople, and wine lovers.

2. **Buying Power.** The second trait that your target market will share is their ability to purchase certain goods and services. This characteristic includes both the consumers' income level and willingness to pay.

   Here's an example: Say there are two Airbnbs in New York City. One is in the West Village in Manhattan while the other is in Jackson Heights in Queens. Since they are both located in New York City, they will likely have the same target market. However, even if their target market has the same level of income, guests will be willing to pay more for the Airbnb in West Village because of its good location.

   Your consumers' buying power also gives you insight into the demand in the market. If your consumers' buying power is high, then you can increase your rate per night until you reach price equilibrium. Again, we're going back to the fundamental economic principle of supply and demand.

3. **Demographics.** Lastly, your target market will share the same demographics. Are you marketing to young people? Families? Businesspeople? Depending on your location, you will attract tourists of a certain age, gender, income level, job or industry, etcetera.

You need to figure out who your target market is so you can concentrate your marketing efforts and prepare your property accordingly. If your target market is families, your place should be child-friendly. If it is businesspeople, you must have a desk space where they can work. If they have a high buying power, your place should look luxurious and high-end to fit the rate you're charging.

Customer Avatar

Aside from finding similar characteristics within your target market, you can get to know your potential guests better by creating a customer avatar. A customer avatar is a detailed profile of who your ideal customer is. Unlike your target market, this focuses on one specific customer and what characteristics you think or want them to have. You need this tool to personalize your product development and content marketing. It also allows you to improve guest experience when you start welcoming people into your home. Lastly, it helps you create a more distinct brand for your Airbnb.

Creating a customer avatar has five parts:

1. **Personal Information.** This step includes your ideal customer's age, gender, marital status, number and age of children (if any), location, job or industry, income level, and other details that may affect their interests and buying power. I also like to include a short quote that I think encapsulates the personality of my ideal customer.

2. **Goals and Values.** What goals and values does your ideal customer have? Are they goal-driven or free-spirited? Do you want their values to be in line with yours? These factors will greatly influence how you set up your Airbnb and what rules you're going to impose on guests.

3. **Challenges.** What challenges is your ideal customer possibly facing? How can you help them overcome these challenges? Since you're offering a short-term housing solution, you should list challenges that are related to the hospitality industry, e.g. places to visit, good restaurants around town, nice and comfortable stay, etcetera.

4. **Roles.** What roles does your ideal customer play in the success of your business? There's an obvious answer to this question—reviews. Guests will leave reviews on your Airbnb listing if they are satisfied or not with the service you're offering. However, you may also be looking for guests that will fill other roles. For example, companionship and friendship. Do you want to socialize with your guests while they're staying at your place? You should indicate this in your customer avatar as well.

5. **Sources of Information**. What books, magazines, websites, podcasts, and other sources of information can you access to help you cater to your ideal customer's needs?

To illustrate what a customer avatar looks like, let's take San Francisco as an example. Let's say there is one host who has a three-bedroom apartment in the city. We'll call him Mike. He wants to rent out his spare bedrooms and to customize each space for his ideal customers. His customer avatars will look like these:

If you're listening to the audio version of this book, you will have access to the PDF of this book that will include the chart below:

Customer Avatar: Visual Artist

Property: Private bedroom in a three-bedroom apartment

Goals and Values	Personal Information	Sources of Information
Goals: • Create art that has socio-political significance • Use their talents to inspire others • Find creative inspiration while in the city Values: • Committed to their art and cause • Friendly and personable • Not pretentious	Age: 24-34 Gender: Any Marital Status: Single Children: None Location: United States Industry: Creative Annual Income: $60,000 Others: Likes to go out and explore the city to find	Books: • *Raise the Bar* by Jon Taffer • *Legal Guide for the Visual Artist* by Tad Crawford • *Picture This: How Pictures Work* by Molly Bang Podcasts: • *Hotel Design*: What I've Learned hosted by Stacy Shoemaker • *The Artist Next Level*

	inspiration for their creative projects. Quote: "Everything you can imagine is real." —Pablo Picasso	hosted by Sergio Gomez • *The Art Angle Podcast* by artnet News
Challenges • Needs a space to work on their project • Have been to San Francisco before but is always looking for new galleries and places to visit		**Roles:** • Leave at least a 4.5-star review so I can maintain my Superhost status • Have a conversation with them

Customer Avatar: Coder		
Property: Private bedroom in a three-bedroom apartment		

Goals and Values	Personal Information	Sources of Information
Goals: • Create an app that makes life easier for a lot of people • Found a startup in the next few years • Find a new job in Silicon Valley while in the city Values: • Passionate and dedicated to their work • Eager to find like-minded people	Age: 22-24 (fresh grad) Gender: Any Marital Status: Single Children: None Location: United States Industry: Technology	Books: • *The Execution Factor: The One Skill that Drives Success* by Kim Perell • *What is Coding?* by Steffi Cavell-Clarke and Thomas Welch • *Zero to One: Notes on Startups, or How to Build the Future* by Peter Thiel, Blake Masters, et al. Podcasts: • *InnSpeaker Podcast* hosted by

- Striving for success and excellence	Annual Income: $60,000 Others: Always working on their computer but still likes to socialize	Matthew Brown and Timothy Resnik - *This Week in Tech* hosted by Leo Laporte - *Tech News Briefing* by the Wall Street Journal
Challenges - Needs a quiet space to work - First time in San Francisco, needs a guide to explore the city	Quote: "Technology is unlocking the innate compassion we have for our fellow human beings." —Bill Gates	**Roles:** - Leave at least a 4.5-star review so I can maintain my Superhost status - Learn something new about the tech industry from them

Can you imagine how you'll design your space for customers like these? Each room can be designed according to each ideal customer. Mike can put artsy decor pieces in the artist's room and technology-themed pictures in the coder's room. He should also put a desk in each room if the ideal guests are young professionals. Plus, he should tailor his guide to San Francisco, if he's providing one, according to what these guests might like. The guide can include galleries for the artist and coffee shops that are conducive for work. And because Mike wants to socialize with his guests, he should make his living space look inviting so that guests will not stay inside their rooms the whole time.

Even though not all customers will be exactly the same, a customer avatar will still help you prepare instead of going into this endeavor blindly. You can anticipate a potential guest's needs and go out of your way to make their stay as comfortable, enjoyable, and sociable as can be.

Housekeeping

In the previous chapter, we talked about how your action plan should include a check-in checklist so you can properly prepare your Airbnb before new guests arrive. One of the items on this list is housekeeping. However, before you even post your listing on Airbnb, you should prepare your property by cleaning it out and making sure that it is suitable for guests.

Housekeeping will not look the same for everybody. It will depend on the size and amenities of your property as well as other factors. But there are regular house cleaning tasks that all hosts should perform before accepting bookings and welcoming new guests.

Here's a housekeeping checklist that everybody can use:

If you're listening to the audio version of this book, you will have access to the PDF of this book that will include the chart below:

Tasks		Done? (Y/N)
Clean	<ul><li>showers and tubs</li><li>toilets</li><li>sinks</li><li>tables</li><li>countertops</li><li>microwaves, ovens, and cooktops</li><li>dishwasher</li><li>refrigerator</li><li>windows</li></ul>	
Disinfect	<ul><li>showers and tubs</li><li>toilets</li><li>sinks</li><li>tables</li><li>countertops</li><li>door knobs</li></ul>	
Vacuum	<ul><li>carpet and hardwood floors</li><li>upholstery</li></ul>	
Change	<ul><li>sheets</li><li>towels</li><li>bath mats</li><li>toilet paper rolls</li><li>toiletries</li></ul>	

	• snacks, coffee, and tea • trash bags	
Dust	• wooden furniture pieces • surfaces • electric fans • blinds and window sills • top of refrigerator	
Others	• make beds • mop tiled floors • remove cobwebs • secure personal belongings • return things in their original order	

You can add or deduct chores from this list. You can also print it out or put it on your phone (for a greener and more convenient option) so you can always refer to it when new guests are checking in.

Before opening your Airbnb, deep cleaning and decluttering your property are recommended. If you're also going to be living in it, you should try to keep common areas as neat as possible. Your home should still feel like home, only more presentable and put together so that guests don't feel like they're intruding in your space.

Problems and Repairs

When you perform a deep cleaning and decluttering of your property, you may find problems that need to be fixed. These problems can be as simple as fixing broken door knobs, changing light bulbs, or repairing a wobbling chair. However, these problems can also be as serious as repairing your heating and air conditioning systems, interior plumbing and electrical systems, and home's structural components.

I recommend that you do a proper home inspection to identify repairs that need to be made. Before you post your listing, you need to make sure that the quality of your Airbnb is good enough to accommodate guests who are paying to stay here. If not, you can't expect them to leave a good review on your listing. Leaving these problems unsolved will lead to unsatisfied customers and losses in the long-run.

Here's a general list of things you need to inspect around your home:

- smoke detectors

- carbon monoxide detectors

- fire extinguisher

- pests (ants, roaches, or mice)

- heating system

- air-conditioning system

- drainage

- interior plumbing

- electrical system (including light sources)

- structural components (if applicable, e.g. roof and foundation)

- paint job

- doors and windows

- furniture pieces

- appliances

Like the housekeeping checklist, you can add or deduct items from this list depending on what your property has or lacks. If you want to ensure that everything is in good condition, you can hire a professional home inspector before posting your listing.

Interior Design

Not all Airbnb hosts will have the same resources to decorate their space. In fact, most of you who are reading this book are looking for additional sources of income. Unless you're charging hundreds of dollars per night, there's no need to decorate your Airbnb lavishly. You don't really have to aim for luxury because, at the end of the day, you're not running a hotel.

In this section of the chapter, I want to give you eight tips on how to decorate your Airbnb for maximum ratings without breaking the bank.

1. **Design your space for comfort.** Since you're entering the hospitality industry, your main priority is to provide comfort to your guests. Your space should still

look and feel like home, only more elevated, presentable, and suitable for guests.

Designing for comfort is as easy as decluttering your space so that it doesn't feel cramped and suffocating. You can add a coat hook in the foyer where guests can leave their coats. Putting throw pillows on the couch so the guests can comfortably lounge in the living space is also a cost-effective idea.

You don't have to spend a lot of money to make your Airbnb as comfortable as it can be for guests. You don't need to purchase a weighted blanket for the bedroom or a plush sofa for the living room to achieve this design goal. Simple and personalized touches can bring a lot of comfort into the space. You just have to think creatively. Step into your ideal customer's shoes and think, "What do I need to feel comfortable in this space?"

2. **Choose durable furniture pieces.** Because you're welcoming strangers into your property, you want to invest in durable furniture pieces that can resist wear and tear. This tip is particularly helpful for host who are renting out their entire place on Airbnb. While your guests are staying in your property, you don't know how exactly they're going to use it. So durability is key to ensure that your furniture will stand the test of time.

However, you don't need to purchase antiques or expensive furniture pieces for every room in the house. You can accumulate these items over time. For now, you can aim to find a good compromise between quality and price. For example, in Ikea, you can find furniture pieces that are made of real wood or metal instead of laminate and corrugated cardboard. You can get a Ypperlig coffee table for the same price as a Lack coffee table. Although smaller, the former looks more stylish and is more durable than the latter. Here are other alternatives to the popular Lack coffee table:

○ Vittsjö coffee table

○ Kvistbro coffee table

○ Gualöv coffee table

The last two options double as storage, which is a perfect solution for extra blankets, towels, or sheets that your guests might need during their stay if you have limited storage space in the bedrooms.

3. **Dress up the windows.** This tip is one of the easiest ways to make your space look more decorated and put together. It also gives your guests some privacy from your neighbors. Again, you don't need to spend a lot of money on expensive curtains or window treatments. You can always go for simple and plain white curtains (or something with a little bit of pattern or texture), but if you can get a set of curtains that complement the theme or color scheme of your space, you can make a huge difference.

4. **Dress up the walls.** There are several ways to do this. Here are a few ideas:

○ Hang up a mirror. Your guests can use the mirror to check themselves before heading out the door, plus it can make a space look more spacious and airy. The light will bounce off of it too, so it can add lightness to the room.

○ Create a gallery wall. If you currently don't have posters or pictures to display on your walls, you can look for aesthetically pleasing photos on free photo hosting websites like Unsplash then have them printed at a nearby Walgreens or a similar establishment. A poster-sized print costs about $10. You can get cheap frames from Ikea. To save money, you can display some of the prints using washi tape or binder clips hung on finishing nails. However, these options are less durable and will leave your prints unprotected and prone to tearing. For renters, you can use removable hooks.

○ Create a wall accent with paint. This is an inexpensive way to create a focal point in a room, although it can take some time because you need to let the paint dry between coats. If you're willing to put in the work, there are several ways to go about it. First, you can choose one wall to paint a different color. Second, you can create faux panels on the wall using paint and a few trim pieces. Third, you can dip a brush and dab it on the wall to make a polka-dot pattern. Fourth, you can tape off lines on the wall so you can create a vertical or horizontal pattern, which can make the room feel bigger. Fifth, you can try more complicated designs like a geometric pattern, a lattice pattern, an ombre effect, etcetera.

5. **Add greenery.** Plants give a room more life, both literally and visually. You can create a focal point that brings the eyes up and makes the ceiling look taller by displaying plants on hanging planters. You can put plants with long vines on top of tall furniture pieces and appliances, like bookcases and refrigerators, to create a drapey effect. Moreover, flowers on coffee and dining tables are always a great touch. You can also put small cacti and succulents on nightstands, side tables, desks, floating shelves, and kitchen countertops.

   If you don't have a green thumb or are not able to properly take care of plants, you can always find fake ones that look real in Target, Amazon, or West Elm. There are also great finds in thrift stores, and you can look for trinkets and other cheap decor pieces here too!

6. **Keep the space airy.** It's always fun to decorate a space. But some people don't seem to know where to stop. As a result, they overcrowd the space with decor pieces or put conflicting patterns, textures, and colors that make it look cluttered.

   To start, find inspiration photos on Pinterest and then pick elements that you think you can apply to your space. These photos will be your guide so you don't go overboard with the design. After the initial set up, you should take a lap around the place and edit where it's needed. If the space feels overwhelming, you probably need to adjust your design decisions.

7. **Make the space feel cozy.** Even if you need to keep the space airy, you still want it to feel cozy. To help you achieve this, here are a few tips:

○ Decorate with rugs, especially in the living room and bedrooms. Rugs add comfort and warmth to the feet and make the space look more aesthetically pleasing. However, make sure to choose rugs that you can put in the washer and dryer. This allows you to easily do laundry between bookings in case of spills.

○ Add lighting throughout the space. Lighting can come in the form of lamps, overhead lights, and candles. You can put lamps on desks, nightstands, and side tables. Overhead lights will come in handy in dark corners or rooms without enough sunlight coming through the windows. Meanwhile, candles can go in the bathroom, bedroom, and living room. If you're worried about fire hazard, you can use flameless candles.

○ Decorate your sofa with throw pillows and blankets. Again, no need to spend a lot of money on these things. There are cheap options both online and in stores.

8. **Choose simplicity over Instagrammability.** Some Airbnb hosts take simplicity too far and leave their spaces too bare to feel like home. As a result, their chances of getting booked again by the same guests are not as high as those with beautifully decorated spaces. Your space should make guests want to come back to your Airbnb whenever they're in town.

The rule of thumb when decorating your Airbnb is to keep it simple. Because you need to do housekeeping between bookings, you want your job to be as easy as possible. However, don't mistake simple for boring. Even though you want to make your space feel airy, you still want it to look good.

Amenities

You should provide basic amenities that your guests expect to find in every Airbnb so they can have a comfortable experience. These essentials include a toilet paper roll, hand and body soap, a towel and a pillow for each guest, and linens for the bed. For extended stays, you can provide additional supplies for each of these items so that guests can stay comfortable until checkout. Other tangible amenities include the following

- TV
- washer and dryer
- kitchen
- air conditioning
- heating and/or fireplace
- WiFi
- hair dryer
- iron
- smoke detector
- carbon monoxide detector
- baby items (crib and high chair)
- workspace

According to Airbnb, the top five amenities that guests around the world are looking for include air conditioning, pool, kitchen, free parking, and pet-friendly (Airbnb, 2018). If your property has these amenities, your chances of getting booked are higher. However, you don't necessarily have to have them. It is still possible to be a successful Airbnb host without all or any of these amenities.

Depending on your ideal customer, you may also decide to provide additional amenities, like toys or a play area for children, free Netflix access, a welcome basket, a charging station for devices, etcetera. You can charge more per night for these amenities because they increase your hospitality as a host and improve the experience for guests.

In addition, your property may also have facilities that guests are looking for, which include a free parking space, a gym, a hot tub, and a pool. You should indicate in your listing all of the amenities and facilities that your property has. Airbnb has a filter system that allows guests to search for amenities and facilities that they want to have on the property. This makes it easier for guests to find your property on the website and app.

Inventory

Kenton (2019b) identifies inventory as "goods available for sale and raw materials used to produce goods available for sale." However, as an Airbnb host, you're not actually selling goods or raw materials. You're providing a service. Still, you need to keep a record of your inventory to protect yourself from losses that may occur. Let me elaborate.

Although hosting on Airbnb is a lucrative source of income, you're also opening yourself to certain risks. By letting strangers into your property, you're already faced with a major dilemma—can you trust this person? After all, you're not running a hotel with a security team on standby. Some of you will be sleeping under the same roof with strangers, while others will let their guests use their entire property without supervision. I'm not sure which scenario causes more uncertainty, but you should know that this feeling is completely normal.

In fact, Gebbia (2016) told a story during his TedTalk about the difficulties they faced when approaching investors at the early stages of their business. He said, "No one in their right minds would invest in a service that allows strangers to sleep in people's homes. Why? Because we've been taught as kids, strangers equal danger."

However, even though strangers pose danger, there's no need to panic because Airbnb actually has a four-fold host protection system in place to make you feel safe. It includes:

1. **Guest reviews.** Guests can leave hosts reviews and vice versa. This two-way review system encourages good service from the hosts, good behavior from the guests, and transparency on both sides. Before you confirm a booking, you can check the reviews that previous hosts have left on the guest's profile.

2. **Internal communication.** You can directly communicate with the guest through Airbnb's website and app. This allows you to ask potential guests some questions before you confirm their booking. You can also request requirements, clarify house rules, and set expectations during your initial conversations with potential guests.

3. **Booking requirements.** To feel more comfortable letting strangers stay in your home, Airbnb allows you to

ask for the following requirements from guests before you confirm their booking:

- ○ verified phone number,

- ○ government-issued ID,

- ○ agreement to house rules,

- ○ a conversation with the guest, and

- ○ positive reviews and good ratings from previous hosts.

4. **House rules.** Speaking of house rules, you can set guidelines that guests must read and agree to follow before you confirm their booking. If they break one of the rules, Airbnb allows you to cancel their reservation (Airbnb, n.d.c).

Another way to protect yourself from losses and damages is to keep an inventory of your assets, especially big ticket items like electronics and appliances. You can refer to your list when you do housekeeping between guests to make sure that everything is still in place. If a guest steals, say, a towel, you can reach out to them politely and ask if they had taken the item by mistake. If they are unresponsive or deny the allegation even after you've provided proof, you can leave them a bad review. You can also give them a low rating if they caused minor damages (like breaking a lamp) and fail to inform you about it.

For bigger damages and theft of more expensive items, like your television and other appliances, you can call the cops, hire a prosecutor, and make a claim. Unfortunately, this kind of problem is a possibility when you open your home to strangers. For example, a man named Martin Irwin gave a fake name to rent an Airbnb in Edmonton, Canada. He stole and left damages worth $50,000 to the property (Bench, 2019).

The good news is that Airbnb has another layer of protection for when this kind of unfortunate event happens. Airbnb's Host Guarantee offers up to a million dollars of property damage protection to every host and each of their listings. This comes completely free with every booking and covers damages to the property. However, their property damage protection is not an insurance policy and has certain limitations and exemptions, which you can find on the website (Airbnb, n.d.d). An inventory will help you write a detailed report of what has been stolen or damaged. You can also provide it to the cops if an investigation is deemed necessary.

Aside from your assets, you should also keep an inventory of the amenities you're providing so you don't run out of supplies. For the sake of our current discussion about inventory, we will define amenities as items that you provide to guests during their stay, while assets are items that are included in the property.

Below is an example of what an assets inventory looks like. This is for a host with a two-bedroom apartment who rents out the guest bedroom on Airbnb. I filled out the first section for the living room to give you an idea of what this would look like. The remainder are for you to complete!

If you bought the audio version of this book, you will have access to the free PDF of the book where you can look at this chart:

Assets Inventory (by room)		
Quantity	Item	Brand and Model
Living Room		
1	Sofa	Ikea Sandbacken sleeper sectional
1	Coffee table	Ikea Hemnes coffee table
2	Side tables	Homfa nesting coffee end tables
2	Lamps	Ikea Fado table lamp
1	Bookcase	Ikea Hemnes shelf unit
1	Television	Samsung UN58RU7100FXZA
1	TV console	Ikea Hemnes TV unit
8	Pillows and pillow covers	- (4) Phantoscope throw pillow inserts - (4) WLNUI throw pillow covers
10	Picture frames	Americanflat 10-piece photo frame pack
7	Plants	- (3) cacti - (2) succulents - (2) snake plants
14	Decor pieces	- (1) Mkono moon phase garland - (5) Mkono planters - (2) Exquis Home ceramic pots

		- (1) MainEvent letter board - (2) Ambipolar cat bookends - (3) Luminicious flameless candles
7	Books	- *Looking for Alaska* by John Green - *Becoming* by Michelle Obama - *The Subtle Art of Not Giving a F*ck* by Mark Manson - *Yes Please* by Amy Poehler - *Lord of the Flies* by William Golding - *The Book Thief* by Markus Zusak - *Blink* by Malcolm Gladwell
Kitchen/Dining Room		
...	...	...
Kitchenware/Houseware		
...	...	...
Master Bedroom		
...	...	...
Guest Bedroom		
...	...	...

As you can see, I suggest that you keep a separate list for kitchen/dining room items and kitchenware/houseware. The former will contain furniture pieces and big appliances, while the latter will contain smaller appliances and other items.

Now, let's take a look at what an amenities inventory looks like. This is for the same host as above, and he is hosting a couple for four nights.

Amenities Inventory (by category)		
Item	For use	In storage
Toiletries		
Toilet paper	3	9
Hand soap	1	5
Body wash	2	10
Shampoo	2	10
Conditioner	2	10
Towel	2	4
Robe	2	4
Toothpaste	1	5
Toothbrush	2	10
Food		
Coffee	4	16
Tea	4	16

Chips	4	8
Salt	1	1
Ketchup	1	1
BBQ Sauce	1	1
Mustard	1	1
Miscellaneous		
Uno Game	1	0
Checker Board	1	0
Paper towels	5	5
Dish soap	1	1

As you can see, I suggest that you create two columns for items that are out for guests to use and those that are still in storage. The quantities for the "For use" column will change depending on the number of guests for each booking, while the "In storage" column will change as your supplies get depleted.

For your amenities, I also recommend putting extra toiletries in the guest bedroom (the quantity will depend on how many nights the guests are staying in your Airbnb, toothbrush excluded) and to keep the rest in a locked cupboard to prevent petty theft. You should check this list regularly to know if you need to shop for supplies before a guest arrives.

Dry Run

In research, a dry run is called a pilot study, and it is defined as:

> a small study to test research protocols, data collection instruments, sample recruitment strategies, and other research techniques in preparation for a larger study. [It] is one of the important stages in a research project and is conducted to identify potential problem areas and deficiencies in the research instruments and protocol prior to implementation during the full study (Hassan, Schattner & Mazza, 2006).

In the hospitality industry, the dry run aims to achieve the same outcomes. You perform a dry run so you can test protocols and strategies, collect data, and prepare for the actual opening of your business. This gives you time to identify problems so you can fine-tune your protocols, strategies, and instruments before you welcome real guests to your home. In addition, a dry run will help you:

- get familiar with your procedures,

- perform a feasibility analysis,

- create a protocol that is applicable to most, if not all, bookings,

- come up with solutions for possible challenges, and

- make adjustments to your action plan, customer avatars, inventory, and other business aspects if necessary.

Phase I: Before

There are three stages to the first phase of the dry run: creating a questionnaire, recruiting participants, and preparing the property. We're going to discuss each stage of the pretrial phase. In particular, what questions do you need to include to the questionnaire. How do you recruit participants that will give you an accurate idea of how your Airbnb will perform? What do you need to do to prepare the property before each booking?

1. **Create a questionnaire.** You need to create a questionnaire that you can hand out to participants so you have a standardized assessment procedure. This also allows participants to give a detailed account of their experience.

   The questionnaire should have three parts. First, participants need to evaluate you as the host. Second, they need to evaluate the property and the quality of stay it provides. Lastly, they will give you suggestions on how you can further improve the experience. You will give this questionnaire to participants during the final phase of the dry run. Here is a sample questionnaire.

If you bought the audio version of this book, you will have access to the free PDF of the book where you can look at this questionnaire:

Airbnb Dry Run Questionnaire

Part I. Host

From a scale of one (lowest) to five (highest), please rate the following experiences:

1. Communication   1   2   3   4   5

2. Personality   1   2   3   4   5

3. Hospitability   1   2   3   4   5

Part II. Airbnb

From a scale of one (lowest) to five (highest), please rate the following experiences:

1. Booking   1   2   3   4   5

2. Check in   1   2   3   4   5

3. Check out   1   2   3   4   5

From a scale of one (lowest) to five (highest), please rate the following aspects of the Airbnb:

1. Cleanliness   1   2   3   4   5

2. Orderliness	1	2	3	4	5
3. Decor	1	2	3	4	5
4. Comfort	1	2	3	4	5
5. Amenities	1	2	3	4	5
6. Facilities	1	2	3	4	5
7. Location	1	2	3	4	5
8. Accessibility	1	2	3	4	5

Part III. Suggestions

How can the host improve your experience?

_____

_____

_____

_____

Pro Tip: You can also leave this questionnaire for real guests to answer if they prefer before they check out.

This will give you an opportunity to further improve your amenities, hosting skills, and Airbnb as a whole.

2. **Recruit participants.** You need to look for the following qualifications when looking for participants:

   a. Your candidates must be from your target market, i.e. have the same geographical interest, buying power, and demographics.

   b. Your candidates must resemble your ideal customer, i.e. have most, if not all, characteristics that you listed in the customer avatar.

   c. Your candidates must have little or no bias. The participants must not sugarcoat their comments and suggestions during Phase III of the dry run. They should be able to tell you if they have noticed any problems or give you suggestions on how to improve them. For instance, you don't want your mom to participate in the dry run if she has a sweet and gentle demeanor. You're relying on your participants' transparency to ensure the success of the dry run.

If you can find candidates that pass these three qualifications, you should ask them to participate in the dry run. I recommend that you also perform a dry run for someone who is not part of your target market and another who does not fit your customer avatar. When you open your Airbnb, you will surely encounter these kinds of customers, and you want to be prepared for them as well.

3. **Prepare the property.** You need to prepare your property for the dry run as if you're accommodating paying guests in your Airbnb. This gives your participants an accurate experience so they can also give you accurate ratings. Remember that the dry run is a simulation of your actual process, and preparing your property is a part of that. So clean and stage your Airbnb to   impress the participants. Housekeeping and decorating are part of this step.

Phase II: During

The second phase of your dry run also has three stages: check in, guest stay, and check out. We're going to talk about each phase of the trial proper. In particular, how will guests check in? What can you do to make their stay as enjoyable and comfortable as it can possibly be? Lastly, what do you hope will your guests take away from the experience after they check out?

1. **Choose a check in method.** You can choose between two methods. You can either go the traditional way, i.e. give the guests a key, or you can invest in a keyless door lock. For the latter, you have a few options to choose from, but we'll discuss them later on. For now, let's talk about the differences between these two methods.

   The latter is, in my opinion, better than the former for several reasons, including the following:

   ○ You can say in your listing that self check in is available. You will not have to meet guests when they arrive, which is a great option for those whose properties are scattered all over the country.

○ You don't need to worry about lost keys, so you will not have to worry about those lost keys getting in the wrong hands either.

○ You can always change the code for added safety. On the other hand, changing door locks is a hassle if the guest loses the key.

The only downside I see in smart locks is you need to buy one if don't already have one, and the best keyless door locks can be expensive. However, if you're thinking long term, this is actually a good investment for you because you and your guests are going to be using it for a really long time.

As for the types of keyless door locks, there are some with number pads, so you can create a code, which is usually four to six digits long. Others are compatible with virtual assistants like Amazon Alexa and Google Assistant. There are also keyless door locks that you can control on your smartphone, so you can change the combination immediately if there is any danger. Meanwhile, some have a built-in alarm system so you can be warned if someone is trying to guess the combination. You can also choose between battery-operated and plug-in keyless door locks. The choice is totally up to you.

To help you make a decision, though, here are some of the best keyless door locks that are currently on the market:

○ Schlage Z-Wave Touchscreen Keypad Smart Lock (compatible with Amazon Alexa and Apple HomeKit)

○ August Smart Lock Pro and Connect Bundle (compatible with Amazon Alexa, Google Assistant, and Apple HomeKit)

○ SkyBell HD Smart Lock (compatible with IFTTT and Amazon Alexa)

Runners-up include the Nest X Yale Keypad Smart Lock, the Schlage Encode Smart Lock Wi-Fi Deadbolt, and the Kwikset Kevo Smart Lock Bluetooth Deadbolt.

2. **Give guests the best stay.** Hopefully, with all the preparations you've made before the dry run, your participants will have the best time while staying in your Airbnb. After all, their experience will give you insight as to how real guests will react to the place.

There's not much you can do at this stage, except to inform your guests that your line of communication is always open. If they have questions or requests, make sure to respond to them as soon as possible.

3. **Keep hosting until check out.** Even after your guests have left your Airbnb, there are still a few things that you need to do. For instance, you should remember to send them a message, thanking them for choosing your Airbnb and reminding them to leave you a positive review if they liked the experience. You should also leave with a call-to-action that proposes re-booking in the future. Here is an example:

"Thank you for staying with me during your trip! I hope you had a lovely stay. If you enjoyed the experience, please don't forget to leave me a review on the Airbnb website or app. Your comments and suggestions are greatly appreciated. Have a safe trip back home, and I hope to see you again!"

Of course, after the participants check out, you should also simulate other tasks like taking inventory and checking if there are any lost items or damages to the property. If you have another dry run round with another set of participants, you should transition back to Phase I, specifically the last step in this phase. You will only move on to the last phase of the dry run once all of your participants have stayed in your Airbnb.

Phase III: After

There are only two stages in the last phase of the dry run: assessing the test and making adjustments. Here is what each stage entails:

1. **Assess the success of the dry run.** You can do this by asking your participants to answer the questionnaire that you prepared during the first phase. You can also conduct interviews to have a full grasp of their experience.

2. **Make necessary adjustments.** Based on the results of the survey, you can formulate changes to make everything run smoother when you open your Airbnb for real. If the check in process scored low, then maybe you need to change your current method. However, if location or accessibility didn't have a great score, you

can't really move your Airbnb to another spot in the city. What you can do is to compensate by providing a guide showing guests nearby hidden spots that they can visit (aside from the popular tourist spots) during their stay. You can also provide them with a list of numbers they can call if they need car service or want to rent vehicles.

Action Plan

Before we close this chapter, let's talk about creating an action plan that outlines your pre-opening strategy. This action plan is different from the one we discussed earlier in Chapter 1. This focuses on how you can effectively prepare your property for the opening of your Airbnb.

Like the previous section, this action plan has three phases: customer, property, and dry run. We'll discuss each phase and the steps you need to complete before you move on to the next one.

Phase I: Customer

The first phase of your pre-opening strategy focuses on your potential customers. There are only two steps in this phase:

1. **Analyze your target market.** Why are potential customers traveling to your vicinity? What is their buying power? What are their demographics?

2. **Create a customer avatar.** Who is your ideal customer? What are their goals and values? What challenges can you help them overcome? What is their role in the success of your business? What sources of

information can you use to know them better and prepare for their stay?

Phase II: Property

The second phase of your pre-opening strategy focuses on your property. It is the bulk of your action plan. There are six steps in this phase:

1. **Perform housekeeping practices.** These include decluttering and deep cleaning your property so it is suitable for guests.

2. **Identify problems that need to be repaired.** If there is anything broken in your property that will affect the quality of your guest's stay, you need to get it fixed before opening your Airbnb.

3. **Design your property.** In an earlier section of this chapter, I gave you eight tips on how to design your property to get more bookings and receive higher ratings. These include designing for comfort, choosing durable furniture pieces, dressing up the windows and walls, adding greenery, keeping the space airy, making the space feel cozy, and choosing simplicity over Instagrammability.

4. **Provide amenities.** There are basic amenities that are essential in any Airbnb. But if you include additional amenities that make your guests feel more comfortable during your stay, you improve customer satisfaction, ensure good reviews, and increase re-bookings.

5. **Keep an inventory.** You need to keep two inventory lists, i.e. one for assets (items that come with the property) and another for amenities (items that you provide to make guests comfortable). These lists allow you to check if anything has been stolen after a guest checks out, assess damages if there are any, file a detailed report if needed, issue a claim to your insurance provider or Airbnb's Host Guarantee protection, and restock when your supplies are running low.

Phase III: Dry Run

The last phase of the pre-opening strategy only has one step: the dry run. However, as you have learned from the preceding section of this chapter, the dry run is actually a complicated process because you're simulating the actual experience. You also need to conduct an assessment once it is done, so you can make adjustments if necessary.

Chapter 3: How to Create and Optimize Your Listing

Once you've prepared your property and made it suitable for guests, your next step is to create and optimize your listing to maximize views, inquiries, and bookings. In this chapter, we'll discuss the five things you need to know about Airbnb listings: signing up, copywriting, photography, ranking, and refining.

In particular, we will answer the following questions: How do you sign up to Airbnb? How do you craft a listing title and write up that captures your target market's attention? How do you take photos that make customers more interested to book your place? How can you improve your search results ranking? Finally, how can you refine your listing to improve your statistics in the future?

Signing Up

The sign-up process is more than just joining Airbnb as a host. You also have to set rates and available dates, request guest requirements, and create house rules. We'll talk about each of these steps in this section of the chapter.

Setting Up Account

When you create an account on Airbnb, you can choose to do it with your Facebook, Google, or email account. The first two options will speed up the process, but you have to allow Airbnb to access certain information from these websites. If you choose the last option, you'll have to provide your email address, first and last name, and birthday. You will also have to create a password with at least eight characters containing a number or a symbol.

After creating your account, Airbnb will require you to provide more information by asking the following questions:

1. **What kind of place do you have?** You need to indicate if you're renting out the entire place, a private room, or a shared room. You also need to disclose how many guests (between one to 16) will comfortably fit in your Airbnb. Lastly, you need to provide the location of your Airbnb. In succeeding questions during the sign-up process, Airbnb will ask for the same details just to clarify the capacity of your property. You'll see what I mean later on.

2. **What kind of place are you listing?** You need to indicate what kind of property you have. Is it an apartment, a house, a secondary unit, a unique space, a bed and breakfast, or a boutique hotel? After choosing a primary category, Airbnb will require you to be more specific in terms of the type of property. Refer to the end of this section to see all of the property types that you're allowed to list on Airbnb. After providing this information, you'll have to indicate what guests will have in the property (entire place, private room, shared room), if the space is dedicated to guests or if you'll be keeping personal belongings in it, and if you're listing on Airbnb as part of a company.

3. **How many guests can your place accommodate?** How many beds can guests use? How many bedrooms are in the property and which beds are in them? You also need to indicate what kind of bed is in each

bedroom and/or common space. Refer to the table at the end of this section for a list of available sleeping arrangements you can list.

4. **How many bathrooms?** Bathrooms without a shower or a bathtub are considered half bathrooms. You also need to indicate if the bathroom is private or shared.

5. **Where's your place located?** You need to indicate the country/region, street address, city, state, and zip code of your property. The next step will require you to confirm if the pin on the map is in the right location.

6. **What amenities do you offer?** Aside from basic amenities, you should also list safety amenities that your property has. Refer to the table at the end of this section to see a list of basic and safety amenities that you can include in your listing. Once your listing is published. you can add more amenities that may not be included in the initial list so you can attract more views, inquiries, and bookings on Airbnb.

7. **What spaces can guests use?** Your property may have additional spaces that can attract potential guests. You will find a list of what these spaces are in the table on the next page.

If you bought the audio version of this book, you will have access to the free PDF of the book where you can look at this chart:

Airbnb Listing Information	
Properties	
Apartment	Apartment Condominium Casa Particular (Cuba) Loft Serviced Apartment
House	House Bungalow Cabin Casa Particular (Cuba) Chalet Cottage Cycladic House (Greece) Dammuso (Italy) Dorne House Earth House Farm Stay Houseboat Hut Lighthouse Pension (South Korea) Shepherd's Hut (UK, France) Tiny House Townhouse Trullo (Italy) Villa
Secondary Unit	Guesthouse Guest suite Villa

Unique Space	Barn
	Boat
	Bus
	Camper/RV
	Campsite
	Castle
	Cave
	Dorne House
	Earth House
	Farm Stay
	Houseboat
	Hut
	Igloo
	Island
	Lighthouse
	Pension (South Korea)
	Plane
	Shepherd's Hut (UK, France)
	Tent
	Tiny House
	Tipi
	Train
	Treehouse
	Windmill
	Yurt
Bed and Breakfast	Bed and Breakfast
	Casa Particular (Cuba)
	Farm Stay
	Minsu (Taiwan)
	Nature Lodge
	Ryokan (Japan)
Boutique	Boutique Hotel

Hotel	Aparthotel
	Heritage Hotel (India)
	Hostel
	Hotel
	Nature Lodge
	Resort
	Serviced Apartment
	Kezhan (China)

Sleeping Arrangements

Bed	King
	Queen
	Double
	Small Double
	Single
	Bunks
Mattress	Floor Mattress
	Air Mattress
Children	Crib
	Toddler Bed
Others	Hammock
	Water Bed

Amenities

Basic	Essentials (towels, bed sheets, soap, toilet paper, and pillows)
	Air Conditioning
	Heat
	Hair Dryer

	Closet/Drawers Iron TV Fireplace Private Entrance Shampoo Wifi Desk/Workspace Breakfast, Coffee, Tea
Safety	Lock on Bedroom Door (notable for private rooms in shared spaces) Fire Extinguisher Carbon Monoxide Detector Smoke Detector First Aid Kit
Additional Spaces	
In-unit	Private Living Room Kitchen
Laundry	Laundry — washer Laundry — dryer
In-Building	Parking Gym Pool Hot Tub Elevator

Requesting Guest Requirements

The second step in signing up as an Airbnb host is actually to set the scene, i.e. to post photos, write a short description, and add a title to your listing. However, I decided to give them their own sections in this chapter because they require certain skills that you may need more help in.

For now, let's skip to the third step in the sign-up process, i.e. preparing for guests. The first portion of this step is to review Airbnb's guest requirements to request additional requirements if you please.

Airbnb requires all guests to provide an email address, a confirmed phone number, and their payment information. Before they can book a property, they should also agree to your house rules, send you a message, let you know how many guests are staying at your place, and to confirm their check-in time at least two days before arriving. You can also require guests to send a copy of a government-issued ID and to have recommendations from other hosts (with no negative reviews). These additional requirements will help to put your mind at ease and make you feel more confident in letting strangers stay in your property. However, you should know that more requirements may lead to fewer reservations according to Airbnb.

Creating House Rules

The second portion of the third step in the sign-up process is creating house rules that your guests must agree to follow before they book your property. You need to indicate if your Airbnb is suitable for pets, infants (under two years old), or children (from two to 12 years old). You should also inform guests if smoking is allowed or if they can have events or parties on the property. You may also include quiet hours if your property is located in a neighborhood or building that requires them.

In addition, Airbnb requires you to include details that guests should know about your property before they book it on the platform. These include:

- must climb stairs,

- potential for noise,

- pet(s) live on property,

- no parking on property,

- some spaces are shared,

- amenity limitations,

- surveillance or recording devices on property,

- weapons on property, and

- dangerous animals on property.

Once you've set these house rules, you can also choose to review every booking request. However, you should know that hosts who allow instant booking have higher earnings and receive more views on average.

Setting Rates and Available Dates

The last portion that you need to complete to finish the sign-up process is to set rates and available dates. Before you do this, though, Airbnb will ask you if you have rented out your place before and how often you want to have guests in the property. For the latter, you can choose among three options: not sure yet, part-time, or as often as possible. This allows Airbnb to suggest settings that will help you become more successful on the platform.

Next, Airbnb will ask you several questions about your available dates. These include the following:

1. **How much notice do you need before a guest arrives?** You can choose among five options: same day, one day, two days, three days, or seven days. If you choose at least two days, you'll have plenty of time to prepare your property between guests. You can perform housekeeping tasks, check and/or replenish inventory, and make other preparations. However, you might miss out on last-minute reservations if you choose this option.

   During this step, you should also indicate when guests can check in. You can set a check in time between 8:00 A.M. to 2:00 A.M. (next day) or set it as "flexible" if you have self check in available.

2. **How far in advance can guests book?** There are six options here: dates unavailable by default, three months in advance, six months in advance, nine months in advance, 12 months in advance, or all future dates available.

If you're not sure about your schedule, you should choose "dates unavailable by default" to avoid cancellations from your part. You can later on unblock dates that you're available to host so you prevent conflicts.

3. **How long can guests stay?** You can set a minimum and a maximum number of nights. There are several considerations that you need to think about during this step.

   O Setting your minimum nights at a certain number help ensure that you earn a certain level of income per month through Airbnb. For instance, if your rate is $80 per night and your minimum number of nights is three, that's a gross of at least $240 per guest, which means you only need to book five guests and 15 nights per month to earn a gross of $1200 per month.

   O Increasing your minimum allowable nights also mean that you have to do housekeeping and turnovers less often.

   O However, if you set your minimum allowable nights per month too high, you will not be able to accommodate short trips. If short trips are more popular in your area, then you might not be as successful as other Airbnbs.

   O There is no cap on the maximum allowable nights per month. However, if you have a schedule that changes quite frequently or if you're not yet sure about how often you want to accept guests in your Airbnb, you should set it to a manageable number, like 10 days or less, so you wouldn't have to cancel bookings unexpectedly. You can also change this to seven days for weekly stays or 28 days for monthly stays.

When you've cleared up these details, you will be able to figure out which dates to unblock in the next step.

To complete the process, you need to do four things:

1. **Update your calendar.** If you selected "dates unavailable by default" earlier, you're now able to unblock dates that suit your schedule. Otherwise, you can do the opposite and choose to block dates when you will not be available to host.

2. **Price your space.** Airbnb has a Smart Pricing feature that allows you to stay at a competitive price point when the demand is either low or high. During this step, you will need to set three price points. Airbnb will give you suggestions on what the competitive rate is for each price point but you still get to make the final call.

   ○ Base Price. This is the default nightly rate for when you turn off the Smart Pricing feature. You need to refer to the competitive analysis in your growth plan to decide the best base price for your property, amenities, and location.

   ○ Minimum Price. This is the lowest price you're willing to charge guests per night. Airbnb will use this price to attract more customers when the demand is low, e.g. off season, storm warning, etcetera.

    O Maximum Price. This is the highest price you're willing to charge guests per night. Airbnb will use this price when the demand is high, e.g. in season, event or festival, etcetera.

3. **Give a discount to first guests.** You can choose to give 20% off to the first three guests who book your Airbnb. This promo will get the ball rolling so you can start receiving good reviews and earning through the platform.

4. **Offer discounts for longer stays.** If you're willing to host guests for extended periods of time, you can choose to give a weekly or monthly discount. This encourages travelers to book your Airbnb. It also allows you to minimize turnovers between guests. However, you need to make the right preparations for longer stays. They may require different amenities from shorter-term travelers, like extra toiletries, towels, and sheets.

Once you're through with all of these steps, the sign-up process is complete! However, don't post your listing just yet. You might still benefit from the next two sections in this chapter.

Copywriting

If you look through the listings on Airbnb, you will notice that there's a space for hosts to introduce themselves and talk about their spaces. The text is an important part of your listing because it helps potential guests understand what they can expect when they book your space and what kind of host you are.

However, you only have 500 characters to compose a quick summary of what makes your space special. With this small character limit, how can you highlight the best features of your home? Is it possible to write something that properly describes you and your place? The short answer to the latter question is yes. It is possible. With the following tips, you'll be able to craft a description that will entice guests and increase bookings:

1. **Make each character count.** You want to cover and focus on three topics when you're writing your listing description: the property, the neighborhood, and yourself. First, focus on the property. What amenities and facilities can the guests access? However, you only want to highlight the best amenities and facilities because they will be able to see the others on the rest of the listing. You should talk about the interior decor, too. Is it bohemian, modern, or glam? What kind of vibe does it give off? Also, what kind of person will enjoy your Airbnb? You can refer to your customer avatar to answer this question.

   Next, you want to talk about the neighborhood. What nearby tourist spots can the guests visit during their stay? Are there popular local establishments that they should try out?

   Lastly, you want to quickly reassure your guests that you are a hospitable host. However, you should also start your description with a short introduction of yourself. You'll see what I mean at the end of this section.

2. **Add some character.** Whenever I write something, I want my readers to hear my voice as they read through it, even if they don't know who I am. If I put enough character into the piece, they are able to come up with a voice in their head that matches the personality. This creates a sense of familiarity that makes people more comfortable around me (or at least the piece I've written).

You only have 500 characters to write your description so it's easier to be straightforward and to enumerate what you like best about your property. However, don't make your description boring. You want your personality to shine through even if it's just a quick summary. If potential guests can hear your voice while they read your description, it means you've injected enough character into it. The feeling of familiarity translates into something like, "Interesting. I'm going to book this place," in their minds, which is what you want.

3. **Reduce fluff.** Your initial description will probably be longer than 500 characters but that's okay. You can read through your description and reduce fluff by following these techniques:

   ○ Change the way you phrase things. Instead of saying, "The view of the ocean from the balcony is nice," you can say, "The balcony has a nice view of the ocean."

   ○ Remove repetitive content. If you already said that the balcony has a nice view of the ocean, you don't have to say, "You can enjoy ocean views from the balcony."

○ Avoid adverbs. Instead of saying, "The sunrise and sunset views are spectacularly amazing," you should say, "The sunrise and sunset views are amazing." Spectacular and amazing are synonyms, so adding the adverb is unnecessary. If you think "amazing" doesn't capture just how gorgeous the view is, you can replace it with "spectacular" or other synonyms like "breathtaking" and "magnificent."

○ Combine all three tips. Can you tell me what's wrong with this sentence? "You can walk and quickly get to the beach from the apartment by foot."

It's too wordy, it has repetitive content, and it has an unnecessary adverb. Instead of that, you can say, "The beach is a five-minute walk from the apartment." You save nine characters with this sentence that you can use to highlight other parts of the apartment.

4. **Proofread and edit.** After removing the fluff, you need to proofread your description so you can correct grammatical mistakes and other errors. Do this step at least twice so you're sure that your description is clean.

5. **Get feedback.** Lastly, ask a friend to read your description and to comment on it. A pair of fresh eyes can catch mistakes you might have missed. You can also ask your friend if they think your description is enough to entice potential guests.

Before I show you an example of an effective description, let's first talk about the title. Aside from the cover photo, it's the first thing people will see when they're looking through listings on the website or app. You only have 50 characters for the title, but it should still stand out. Here are a few tips on how to write a catchy Airbnb listing title:

1. Avoid generic words. Words like "nice," "good," and "great" don't add much value to your title. They're not catchy enough to hold someone's attention.

2. Use unique words that clearly describe the property. "Boho chic" is more descriptive than "aesthetically pleasing." "Historic building" paints a prettier picture than "vintage" or "old."

3. Be as informative as you can be. Aside from the aesthetic, you might want to mention that your property is at the heart of the city, that it has a pool, or that it has mountain views. You should also mention the type of property you're renting out.

Now, let me show you what an effective Airbnb copy looks like. Let's go back to Mike for an example. You remember him from Chapter 2, right? He has a three-bedroom apartment in San Francisco. Let's say Mike lives in the Marina District. Here's what his Airbnb copy says:

Private room in boho-chic apt w/ sweet garden view

Hi! I'm Mike, a tech entrepreneur with a passion for hosting! My Airbnb is located in the charming Marina District, known for its lively bar scene and breathtaking view of the Golden Gate Bridge. Your room, which comes with a spacious desk, is in a quiet spot in the apartment. Cafés and restaurants are close by, and popular spots like Crissy Field and Fort Point are a 10-minute drive from here. Breakfast is served every morning at around 8:00. I'm excited to be your host in San Francisco!

When writing your copy, you can also provide more information about your space, availability, and neighborhood, as well as ways to get around your city, in four separate text boxes. These have bigger character limits, so take advantage of the spaces you're provided. However, you should still apply the tips you learned earlier so you can give potential guests relevant information without writing an entire novel about your Airbnb.

Photography

Photos are an important element of your listing. They catch the attention of potential guests and may even give you competitive edge. Photos help customers understand why you're charging a certain rate per night. They also help convince customers to book your place given its interior decor, amenities, facilities, spaciousness, and layout.

In this section, we will talk about how you can take photos for your listing using your phone. This device is literally all you need to produce high-quality pictures that will increase your booking rate.

Finding Inspiration

Before you take photos, go online and look for inspiration. All you need are relevant keywords such as "residential architecture," "interior design," and "bedroom goals" to see how professional photographers take pictures of living spaces. You can find inspiration from a lot of places. Google image results have millions of examples, but you can also search for these keywords on Pinterest or Instagram. There are also video tutorials on YouTube that will show you how to take and edit professional-looking pictures on your phone.

Creating a Photo Checklist

Another thing you need to do before you start taking pictures is to create a checklist of what rooms, amenities, and facilities you want to showcase on your listing. The checklist ensures that you've taken all the right pictures to entice potential guests. It also allows you to prepare and stage these rooms, amenities, and facilities so that they'll look their best when you finally take their photos. Be careful not to overdo staging, though. You should prepare them the way you would when you're expecting a guest so that customers will not accuse you of false advertising.

The photo checklist is different for everybody, but to give you an idea of what you should include in yours, here are some rooms, amenities, and facilities that you should have in it:

- bedrooms and sleeping arrangements

- bathrooms

- kitchen and shared spaces

- special amenities (e.g. workspace, bathtub, welcome basket)

- facilities that guests can access (e.g. pool, gym, garden)

- neighborhood and nearby tourist spots

Taking Photos

So how can you take photos that will catch the attention of potential guests? Here are a few photography tips for professional-looking listing pictures using your phone:

- **Take your pictures when the sun is out and bright.** Draw the curtains to the side to let natural light come into the room. Sunlight can do wonders to any picture. While artificial light, especially white light, makes a room feel cold and stony, natural light will make your space feel warm and homey. If your space does not get enough sunlight, you can tag team it with artificial light. Turn on overhead lights and lamps if necessary.

- **Always take pictures on landscape mode.** It will give the guests an idea of how spacious your Airbnb is. Plus, it captures more area in one photo so you don't have to take multiple pictures of one room.

- **Angle your camera towards a corner of the room to improve perspective and depth.** Like taking photos on landscape mode, this angle gives the photo more dimension so that guests can get an idea of how much room there is.

- **Tinker with your phone's camera settings to get the best image quality.** If you have an iPhone, it's as simple as getting the angle you like then tapping and holding the center of the screen until the AE/AF lock is activated. AE/AF means auto-exposure/auto-focus. This feature puts the object of the photo in focus and adjusts the amount of light that the photo receives. (Other phones will have different camera settings and features. Look online for a more comprehensive tutorial on how you can maximize your device's camera).

- **Set the aspect ratio to 3:2 so the photo does not get distorted when you upload it.** Airbnb recommends a minimum resolution of 1024 pixels by 683 pixels, but it will automatically adjust photos that have a much higher resolution than that. Later, in editing, you can choose to downsize your photo to avoid any distortions.

Editing Photos

After taking pictures, select the ones you like the most, so you can begin to edit them. You can use Adobe Photoshop on your computer or different apps on your phone to adjust the exposure, contrast, highlights, shadows, white balance, temperature, saturation, and sharpness of your pictures. Some apps also have presets that you can use so you will not have to manually adjust these settings. If you want to create your own preset, I suggest that you apply the same settings to all of your listing photos so that they will all look cohesive.

Giving advice on how to edit photos is a bit trickier than sharing tips on how to take them because it really depends on how they turned out. However, there is one key rule to editing that you should always keep in mind: don't over-edit your photos! In fact, don't edit them at all if possible. You want your photos to look the same as real life so that guests don't feel misinformed or deceived when they arrive. If you applied the tips from the previous section, you will not need to edit your photos unless you have to crop or resize them.

Before we end this section, I want to answer one question that a lot of Airbnb hosts are asking: "Do I need to hire a professional photographer to take pictures of my space?"

The answer is no. You don't have to. As long as you have a smartphone with a decent camera, there's no point in spending money on a professional photographer. You can take professional-looking photos that will increase your booking rates if you follow the techniques you have learned throughout this section.

Ranking

Most guests will only look through the first few pages of the search results before deciding to book a property. To increase your chances of success on Airbnb, you need to rank higher on the search results page. There are several things you can do to achieve this. Here are seven tips to improve your search ranking:

1. **Write a catchy title and description.** Hopefully, with the techniques that I taught you in the Copywriting section of this chapter, you will be able to come up with a title and description that grabs guests' attention.

2. **Update your listing regularly**, especially when there are new attractions or upcoming events in town. Guests

are not booking your Airbnb just to stay in it. They want to explore the city and experience new things. If they're going to your area for an event, you can describe how close your property is to the venue and suggest other things they can do to maximize their stay.

3. **Set a competitive price.** We already talked about how you can set a competitive nightly rate in Chapter 1. If you offer a great deal on Airbnb, clicks on your listing will increase, which will then improve your ranking based on Airbnb's algorithm.

4. **Respond quickly.** If you always respond to requests within 24 hours, Airbnb's algorithm will favor your listing.

5. **Turn on the Instant Book feature.** Once you get comfortable hosting strangers in your Airbnb, you can further improve your search ranking by allowing guests to book your property instantly because the demand for these listings is higher. If you're not comfortable with this feature, you can certainly keep your listing under the Request to Book category. However, minimize rejections because the algorithm looks into patterns and detects if a host has been turning down guests quite frequently.

6. **Offer discounts for longer stays.** If you want to host guests on a longer-term basis, giving discounts for weekly and monthly stays will also give you an algorithmic advantage.

7. Last but certainly not least, **provide quality service.** Reviews affect your search ranking significantly. If

previous guests are satisfied and pleased with your property and hosting skills, they will be more likely to leave a positive review on your listing. You may also send them a "thank you" message with a gentle reminder to leave you a review after they check out.

Refining

I mentioned in the previous section that you should update your listing regularly. Updating and refining your listing significantly improves your search ranking, which leads to more clicks and bookings. However, there's no need to revise your listing if you're just going to make unnecessary changes. You should only post important information that will help your guests make a decision in your favor. Here are a few examples of what updates will help your listing:

- **Price change.** New hosts are recommended to set their rates a little bit lower than the competitive price so they can start hosting, earning money, and getting positive reviews. Once you've established yourself as a host, you can increase your price.

- **Upcoming events.** Guests traveling to your city may not be aware of an upcoming event that can make their stay either more stressful or more fun. To avoid complaints or to help guests improve their stay, you should inform them of any event that may affect their trip.

- **New amenities or facilities.** These will attract guests to your property like moths to a flame.

- **Renovations.** If you made significant renovations inside your property, you can showcase your new interior by changing the photos on your listing.

- **Seasonal activities.** Is your area known for its summer spots? When winter comes, you can give guests some suggestions on what they can do to maintain a steady number of bookings despite the off-season.

Chapter 4: How to Become a Superhost

Airbnb has a Superhost program that "celebrates and rewards Airbnb's top-rated and most experienced hosts" (Airbnb, n.d.b). To become a Superhost, you need to meet the following requirements:

- complete at least 10 stays in the past year or cumulative 100 nights in at least 3 stays,

- have an average overall rating of 4.8 or higher from guest reviews in the past year,

- have less than one percent cancellation rate (extenuating circumstances excluded), and

- respond within 24 hours to 90% of new messages.

Airbnb Superhosts enjoy exclusive benefits and rewards. In this chapter, you will find out why aiming for that Superhost status is worth it. We will also debunk some myths and answer some frequently asked questions about this coveted title.

Benefits of Superhost Status

There are only four requirements to become an Airbnb Superhost, but it can be difficult to achieve them all at the same time, especially if you're new to hosting on the platform. It will take hard work and dedication for you to achieve the Superhost status. However, there are several good reasons for you to aim for this title, aside from the cool Superhost badge on your profile picture. Here are three awesome perks you'll get to enjoy:

1. **More visibility.** The Airbnb algorithm favors Superhosts and gives them better search rankings. The filter system also has "Superhost" as an option so guests can only see hosts with this status in the search results.

2. **More bookings and bigger earnings.** The Superhost status immediately shows guests that you provide quality service and are trustworthy.

3. **Exclusive rewards.** You will earn a 20% additional bonus for every host referral. You will also receive $100-worth of travel coupons for every year you maintain your Superhost status.

Airbnb Superhost Myths and FAQs

Q: Do I need to apply to become a Superhost?
A: You don't need to apply to become a Superhost. This is one of the myths that a lot of new hosts seem to believe. You just need to focus on meeting all of the requirements because assessments are automatic happen regularly.

Q: How do I track my Superhost status?
A: You can see your progress by going to Performance > Opportunities. Here, you'll see what requirements you've completed or close to completing and what you still need to work on.

Q: How long before I find out if I can become a Superhost?
A: The assessment happens on the first day of January, April, July and October and will take up to two weeks. Every Superhost or candidate will be evaluated during these periods

to see if you've gained, retained, or lost your status. Airbnb will notify you via email.

Q: How long before I can become a Superhost?
A: I've read in multiple Airbnb online forums and communities that a person should be hosting for at least a year before they can become a Superhost. While the Superhost assessment takes into consideration your performance over a 12-month period, you don't need to have hosted for a year to achieve this status as long as you have completed all of the requirements.

Q: What extenuating circumstances allow me to cancel reservations without risking my Superhost status?
A: For every 100 reservations, a host can only cancel one reservation to maintain Superhost status. There are two types of circumstances that qualify hosts and guests for penalty-free cancellations. The first one requires documentation, and it includes the death of the host, immediate family member, or caregiver; unexpected serious illness or injury; government mandated obligations like jury duty, travel restrictions, court appearances, and military deployment; unforeseen property damage, maintenance, and amenity issues; transportation disruptions; and train, bus, or ferry cancellations. The second type requires special review, and it includes natural disasters, terrorist activity, and civil or political unrest; endemic disease or illness; travel restrictions; safety and security threat advisories; essential utility outages; and changes to visa or passport requirements. To file a claim, you need to contact Airbnb within 14 days after canceling the reservation (Airbnb Help Center, n.d.b).

Q: Can I lose my Superhost status?
A: Yes, unfortunately. As I mentioned earlier, Superhost assessments happen on a regular basis, so you need to maintain a good standing.

Chapter 5: How to Automate the Airbnb Process

Nowadays, Airbnb hosts are making their businesses grow by automating certain hosting processes such as check in, communications, and housekeeping. By automating these processes, hosts are able to manage more than one property at the same time without losing their Superhost status. They are able to respond to inquiries and booking requests quicker, improve customer satisfaction, and increase booking rates. Automation also allows them to work full-time while hosting on Airbnb. As a result, they continue earning a steady income from their primary job and maximize Airbnb profits as well. Overall, automation will make you a more efficient host.

This chapter is all about automation. We will talk about what processes you can automate and how you can seamlessly transition into "hands-free" hosting. In addition, I will show you a few tools that you can use for automation. By the end of this chapter, you will have all the information you need to confidently automate your Airbnb, even if you've just started this hosting journey.

Processes to Automate

In my opinion, there are four processes that you should definitely automate to be able to maximize efficiency. They make up more than half of your responsibilities as a host once you start welcoming guests to your property. So I want to focus our discussion in this chapter on these processes. I'll give you actionable steps on how you can automate check in, messaging, housekeeping, and managing multi-listings.

Check In

Airbnb has a very user-friendly way to set up automated check-in through the app. On their website, the instructions are as follows:

1. Go to Your listings on airbnb.com and select a listing

2. Next to Guest resources, click Edit

3. Below Directions, click Add self check-in

4. Select the way that guests can get in to your listing

5. Follow the instructions to add check-in instructions

    Note: We will not show guests these instructions until 3 days before their check-in date. Instructions are saved to the guest's phone and can be viewed even if the phone isn't connected to the Internet (Airbnb, n.d.).

The check in process is the easiest to automate because all you need to do is to invest in and install a smart lock system. You can change the code after every booking. In Chapter 2, we talked about smart locks. I gave you the best products you can buy in the market that will help you automate check in and keep your property secure at the same time. When choosing which one to buy, here are a few things you need to consider:

1. **Installation.** How easy or difficult is it to install? Do you need to hardwire it or is it powered by batteries? If you don't want to go through too much trouble in installing a smart lock or if you don't have electrical

wiring running through your door, then you should get the latter kind.

The problem with battery-operated smart locks, though, is that you will obviously have to change batteries every once in a while. If you have a property in another city or state, this will become a problem. But you can also hire a "handy-man" to manage all your small fixes for properties in other cities as a means of maintaining them and keeping them in working order.

2. **Battery Life.** If you get a battery-operated smart lock, then you want it to consume less power so you will not need to change batteries too often. After all, you're installing it in a rental property that you're planning to automate, so having to change batteries quite often is counterproductive.

There are many factors affecting the power consumption of smart locks. Its connection, for example, is one factor. Typically, Bluetooth and WiFi smart locks consume more power than Z-wave or Zigbee smart locks. But we'll discuss these different types of connection later on.

3. **Compatibility.** When choosing a smart lock, you need to see if it's compatible with your door and smart home system. Some smart locks only work if the deadbolt is mounted and operated independently from the door handle; others work fine with an integrated lock and handle. Some smart locks only work with specific smart home systems, like Amazon Alexa, Google Home, or Apple HomeKit; others are compatible with multiple smart home systems.

However, if you don't have a smart home system in your property, then you don't need to worry about it. You don't have to install a smart home system to be able to operate a smart lock either. Compatibility to smart home systems is completely optional and is only a concern if you already have one in place.

4. **Connectivity.** Smart locks usually operate on four different types of connections: Bluetooth, WiFi, Z-wave, and Zigbee. As I mentioned earlier, the former two consume more power than the latter two, although Bluetooth consumes considerably less power than WiFi.

   In addition, Bluetooth, Z-wave, and Zigbee smart locks have short range connection. But that shouldn't matter too much because you or your guests will not need to unlock the door from afar. Even with an auto-unlock feature (which unlocks the door when it detects your phone, as long as you've downloaded the smart lock app), you want to be standing by the door when it unlocks to avoid security issues.

   Having said all of these, I recommend Z-wave or Zigbee smart locks for Airbnb properties

5. **Convenience.** If your smart lock has an auto-unlock feature, guests may not be able to use it if they don't want to download the smart lock app or if their phones run out of battery. When these happen, they should have another way of unlocking the door. This is when smart lock keypads come in handy.

   At the same time, your convenience matters too. You should be able to configure the lock from your phone so you can change the codes and check the batteries even when you're far away. Some smart locks also have random code generators, so you don't have to come up with new codes every time a guest checks in. You'll be able to access the code through the app or have it sent to you by email or SMS. There are also locks that allow you to set the check-in and check out time and dates. After the check out, the current code will expire so your property stays secure. These features add another layer of automation and convenience for you.

Messaging

You already know that you need to be able to respond to 90% of new messages within 24 hours to keep your Superhost status. By automating responses, you can maintain a good standing even if you can't discuss details with guests at the moment.

I will give you some tools that you can use to be able to automate responses on Airbnb in the next section of this chapter. For now, let's talk about what messages you need to prepare beforehand. These will be sent by the auto-messaging tool once you've set it up. You need to compose five messages: booking confirmation, pre-check in, post check-in, pre-check out, and post-check out.

When composing these messages, be careful not to overdo them. You don't want your message to be too wordy because guests will likely skim it, which can lead to confusion or misunderstanding on their side. Even if it's their fault that they missed an important detail in the message, it will still reflect poorly on you, specifically on their review of you. There, do what you can to avoid this possibility and be as concise as possible. You also want to sound excited about hosting your guests, but not too much that you seem overeager. You don't want to weird them out. In every message, you want to sound professional but hospitable. The key here is to find the right balance between proficiency and friendliness. Below are some templates that you can use for these messages:

Booking Confirmation

> Hello [Guest Name]! Thanks for booking my Airbnb! My name is [Host Name], and I'm really excited to be your host during your stay in [City].
>
> I will send you the check-in information two days before you arrive. This will include the check-in and check-out time, door access code, complete Airbnb address, and other relevant details that will make your arrival more convenient.
>
> If you have any questions or requests, please don't hesitate to send me a message. I will get back to you as soon as possible. Have a nice day!
>
> Thanks,
> [Host Name]

This message is particularly important because, as I've mentioned repeatedly in the past, responding to 90% of new messages within 24 hours is a prerequisite of attaining and maintaining a Superhost status. Although this message plays a huge role in achieving the coveted title, you will notice that it is short and simple but sounds hospitable and friendly at the same time. You earn extra hosting points just by informing the guests that you are open to any questions or requests that they may have.

I also recommend that you inform your guests of when you're going to send them the check-in information so they wouldn't have to ask. This shows your guests that you're able to anticipate their needs, which makes you look like a great host.

Pre-check In Message

> Hi [Guest Name]! Your trip to [City] is just two days away! To ensure a smooth check in, here is everything you need to know.
>
> Your check-in time is at [Check-in Time] on [Check-in Date]. The address is [Complete Address] and the door access code is [Door Code]. Please do not share this code to a non-guest to protect your privacy and safety during your stay. Here are the username and password for the free WiFi:
>
> - Username:
>
> - Password:
>
> On [Check-out Date], your check-out time is [Check-out Time]. If I can help you with anything else, just send me a message. I am more than happy to answer your questions so you can have a five-star stay at my Airbnb.
>
> Thanks,
> [Host Name]

This is another important message to send to your guests, and one that you shouldn't forget to dispatch. The pre-check in message contains important information that your guests will need to be able to actually stay in your Airbnb. Therefore, it is critical that you send this message to the guest when you said you'll send it. If you forget, your guests will feel inconvenienced, which can have a negative effect on their review.

Before guests check-in, you should also send them the house rules. I will not be giving you a template for this because the house rules vary widely among hosts, but I will leave you just one tip: be courteous, clear, and concise.

Post-check In Message

> Good morning, [Guest Name].
>
> I hope you had a great first night in my Airbnb and were able to sleep well. Are you settling in okay? Hopefully, your expectations have been met thus far.
>
> Anyway, I just wanted to check up on you and wish you a great stay for the rest of your trip. As always, if there's anything you need, just let me know.
>
> Thanks,
> [Host Name]

This message is not as important as the first two and is completely optional, but it will make you look like a host who cares about your guests. Don't expect them to respond to this message, though. Most guests ignore the post-check in message. However, this doesn't mean that they don't appreciate the gesture. It will still reflect on your ability and sincerity as a host and will have a positive effect on your review.

Pre-check Out Message

Hello [Guest Name],

Your check out is scheduled tomorrow, [Check-out Date], at [Check-out Time]. The door access code will automatically expire five minutes after, so make sure you've packed all of your belongings before leaving the house. The housekeeping crew will arrive shortly after your check-out to prepare the house for the next guest. I sincerely appreciate your cooperation.

Thanks,
[Host Name]

Reminding your guests to check out on time is a must to prevent any delays in your hosting processes. You can choose to include this pre-check out message in the house rules, especially if your guests are only staying for one to three nights, so you're not bombarding guests with messages during their stay. For longer reservations, though, sending them a pre-check out message at least a day before they leave is necessary.

Post-check Out Message

Hi [Guest Name]!

Thank you so much for choosing to stay at my place during your trip in [City]. I hope you enjoyed your stay and I would be honored if I can host you again in the future.

If your expectations have been met, would you mind leaving me a review? It only takes a minute or two to complete. Your opinions matter to me and, if you see me and my Airbnb fit, a five-star rating will help me continue providing other guests with quality service. Of course, I will also give you a review in return to help you you book other properties on Airbnb.

Thank you once again and I hope you have a safe trip home.

Until next time,
[Host Name]

While all of these templates are helpful, especially if you're renting out the entire place and don't have an opportunity to interact with your guests in person, you should still use your best judgement on whether or not to send them and when to dispatch them. For example, if you're renting out a private bedroom where you live, you don't need to send the post-check in and pre-check out messages. You can simply relay them to the guest so you can also have a conversation with them.

Housekeeping

There are housekeeping services that charge by the hour. If you search "housekeeping services" with your city on Google, you will find millions of results. Some of them are even Google guaranteed, which means the service has passed Google's screening and qualification process. If you're not satisfied with their service, Google will pay you back.

You can hire one of these services, providing the company with a temporary door access code if you have a smart lock system, and schedule housekeeping after every booking. This is one option to automating housekeeping. However, these services can be expensive, especially if you don't have a minimum number of nights per reservation. The expense can really add up and take a huge chunk of your earnings, if not exceed your income.

If you want to semi-automate this process, you can with a smart home system. There are appliances that are compatible with Amazon Alexa, Google Home, and Apple HomeKit, so you can order them to clean your home with preset commands. Once you've commanded the Roomba vacuum to clean your floors, all you have to do is to sit back and relax...or maybe change the sheets and towels while you're waiting.

Multi-listings

With the previous systems in place, it will be much easier to manage multiple listings at the same time. All you have to do is to set up these processes for automation, then they're ready to do their thing. Of course, automation still requires human intervention. The point of all of this is to make management significantly easier for you since you're likely juggling a regular job with hosting on Airbnb, or managing several properties at once.

For multi-listings, there are other processes that you can automate, like keeping track of your reservations. Although Airbnb will send you notifications on your phone if you have the app, you can add an extra layer of reminder by keeping track of your reservations using a cloud-based calendar. You can also use an app to keep your check-in checklist and inventory list accessible at all times. If you have staff members who are helping you manage properties in other states or cities, there is team management software that can help you keep track of everyone's responsibilities even if you're not physically present in the area.

Moreover, there is property management software that allows you to manage listings across different platforms. If you have listings published on websites other than Airbnb, this type of software allows you to manage all of them in one place so you will not have to switch channels every single time.

Team Management

Owning property can be expensive, so when you get the opportunity to do this with somebody else, you should take it. You can have a partner that helps make decisions and you could invest in even more. Unfortunately, having partners can also be risky. You never know if you can fully trust somebody, depending on the relationship that you have. Before Airbnb introduced a new service, many people had to take risky chances when they invested with others.

They would have to share personal information, such as account passwords, which could end up being used against them later on. Now, Airbnb offers a great tool built in that helps property owners work with other partners. They have a great tool that you can use for collaboration. This tool breaks things down really easily so that you can assign different roles to various partners. Not only does this tool allow you to work just with partners that might be investing the property, but you also can link it so that people like cleaners or managers have access to certain information.

You'll be able to see your team and their assignments, as well as the permission they have to make modifications for the property and provided services. You can give different team members the power to change prices or availability, they can look at finances and create reports of earnings, and they might be able to edit other team members abilities.

Some concert listings and also work with guests management. It's all very customizable so you can start at your own convenience. Go to airbnb.com/hosting/teams to get started. You will only be able to access this with your account as a host.

There you'll be able to add different accounts and link them so that you can provide the right jobs and tasks to them. The categories of permissions are:

- basic permissions

- listing management

- guest management

- pricing and availability

- finances

- team management

Only you will be able to:

- have access to every function mentioned above

- edit account details

- edit tax information

- edit payout preferences

- deactivate the team, your account, and close your account

- have access to filing resolution cases

Your team, depending on what you allow them to do, will be able to:

- edit their own login information

- review and edit calendars and listings

- create listings

- set pricing

- update details about listings

- create, adjust, and cancel reservations

- customer service functions

- send messages and offer promotions

- write guest reviews and respond to them

- create and edit prices or discounts

- access the account transaction history

- review earnings overall

- invite and create new team members

These will be based on what you allow them. If you'd prefer, you can simply give visitation access so they still will have to go through you before making any changes. This is great, because it means you will be able to hire the work that you don't have time to do. For those that can't find it in their budget to incorporate more paid employees, you can also find plenty of help from automated tools.

Tools for Automation

These automated tools are important for **increasing efficiency as an AirBNB host**.

As an Airbnb host, you're going to want to make your experience as easy as possible. The more efficient that you are as a host, the more properties you can manage and the more services you can offer to your guests. If you're feeling overwhelmed by all the minor tasks, then you can overlook something and that might lower your rating.

This is especially true for people who are not going to be doing this full time. This might be a side gig, and you don't want it to turn into something that does consume all the free time you have when you're not working your primary job. This is where automation can come in.

In this section we're going to give you the best tools that are going to make this process as quick as possible. You want to make the most of not only your experience as a host and a manager, but you want your guests to get as much from this as possible. The more that you're giving to them, the easier it will be in the long run because these services will become natural and automated. It might seem like a lot to set up in the beginning, but it's a great way to prevent those minor mishaps and mistakes that other hosts have to learn to fix the hard way.

Smart Locks

We already talked about smart locks earlier. You know how they work and what features you need to consider when choosing a smart lock system. To recap, you need to think about how easy it is to install, how long the battery life is, if it's compatible with your door and/or smart home system, what kind of connection it uses, and whether it makes check in convenient for both you and your guest. The best smart locks on the market are:

- the Schlage Z-Wave Touchscreen Keypad

- the August Smart Lock Pro and Connect Bundle

- the Skybell HD Smart Lock

- the Nest X Yale Keypad Smart Lock

- the Schlage Encode Smart Lock Wi-Fi Deadbolt

- the Kwikset Kevo Smart Lock Bluetooth Deadbolt

Airbnb Saved Message Feature

Airbnb has a saved message feature that you can use to save templates so you will not have to retype them every time you need to send your guest a message. Follow these steps to use this built-in feature:

a. Go to your Airbnb hosting account and click the Messages tab.

b. Choose which guest you plan on sending the message to.

c. You will then be able to use a saved message.

d. Pick whichever message you feel comfortable sharing with them.

e. You can edit the message as needed too.

Play around with your templates to find something that you are comfortable with. As you gain experience, it will be easier to work out any kinks and include more important information that might get missed from guest to guest.

Multi-Listing Management

After you've locked down your first property, you might want to start introducing more locations for people to rent out. It's a great way for you to grow your business, and who knows, you might be able to have this be a full time way of making a large amount of passive income. That's usually the end goal for people who begin property investment in the first place.

There are a few things to keep in mind when it comes to multi-listing management. The first, of course, is that having somebody there who can help you will be more beneficial, so that you never overlook anything. You don't want to have 10 different properties and be the only one who puts any effort in.

If you're not investing full time hours into this, you might ignore one location and forget to stock it with items. You might miss messages and reviews or forget to respond to various emails. Managing one property can be tough, but the more you add the more challenges that will come as well. Make sure when you do begin to manage multiple properties, you only use one account. That is one of Airbnb's rules that you agreed to in their terms depending on the location you set up the account.

The restrictions on multiple accounts can vary by location, so check in with where you are specifically, as well as where your properties are. Remember that all properties will not have the same rules. You might have some locations in the West United States, and you might have others in Eastern Europe. Wherever you have these locations, the rules could be completely opposite from each other, so don't assume that all rules apply everywhere.

You also want to make sure that you are responding to all messages. If you want all of these accounts to remain active, you can't ignore them. That's why it can be easier to have one account, but at the same time, you might get confused about various properties when you're responding to multiple people on the same platform at the same time. This is where automated messaging is going to be your best friend.

You can also look into hiring a property management company who would just take a small portion to make sure that all messages are met. It might seem like an extra expense. But if you let a few accounts go without responding to messages, it could end up affecting your business.

If you are going to be multi listing homes, make sure that you either use a third party automated application, you hire a specific property manager, or you commit yourself to this full time. Making one mistake on one property can act like a domino effect and have a negative impact on all of your locations.

Automatic Replies

One of the best tools that you can use for automatic replies is Smartbnb. You can have different kinds of pre-written replies if that's what you want, but you also have to remember that when you are the one automating these responses, sometimes copy and pasting can be tedious.

That's where different apps can come in to help make this process more streamlined. Smartbnb is one artificial intelligent application which can respond to guest's questions. It comes off in a way that is natural, so it doesn't make it seem as though it's a bot, and it has great functions for proper grammar and spelling.

When using Smartbnb, you'll have to make sure that you are adhering to your specific property rules. You're going to go through a training period with this where you teach the AI what your voice might sound like and what your rules might be.

It can help you to be more quick and efficient when talking to guests. This is definitely one of the best apps to use for automatic message responses because it works with the app. When training the app, you can think of every question possible and share the responses you would think are appropriate. If someone might ask, "Can I bring my dog?" you can give it an automated response. Other features you can train it to do are:

- inquiries (approvement and follow-up)

- booking responses

- check-in and follow up questions

- first day check-in procedures

- reviews and ratings

Aside from these, you can train it to have different features as well. It's important to go back and check-in to make sure that it's keeping up with what you want to respond. You can't entirely ignore it. However, it's a great way to make sure you're at least responding to everyone so that no guest goes unnoticed.

Automatic Reviews

Reviews are a very important process of this entire operation. Your guests are going to be looking at your pictures, your information, and your rating. However, the reviews can really be what makes or breaks the choice between you and your closest competition. It's also fair for you to rate your customers. You will not want them to come back if they were incredibly rude and made a mess.

It's important to respond to every single review, even the good ones. After a guest has checked out from their stay, you will have 14 days to review them. Your guests will not be able to read your review until they have posted their own rating. After these 14 days, they will be able to see the review even if they hadn't posted one of their own.

Automated reviews are one of your options too. When you write a review about them, it can prompt them to want to respond and have their own review. They'll notice that you reviewed them, be curious, and be prompted to review you so that they can see what you said. They will also be unable to see the review until they've done this, so even if you do give a bad review, they will not be able to give a bad one as retaliation.

They have a certain window to give a bad review - 14 days - and you can automate your program to post a review 20 seconds before that 14 days ends. This way they will not be able to give a bad review after they've seen that you gave them a negative one.

Keeping up with reviews is essential because when you get more reviews, you'll get more visibility. Other automated review apps include:

- Your Porter

- iGMS

The biggest killer for your page will be having a ton of traffic but no reviews. You might have had 100 bookings but 10 reviews, so it can make new guests skeptical. Responding to negative reviews is important so that you can make sure you are noticing the problems with your location and working on them. Don't take the criticism too hard - it can help you grow to be even better than the rest!

Automatic Sensors

There are a few sensors and other gadgets you can add to your location to make sure you are improving the experience for the guests. When you have up-to-date technology it helps increase the guest's experience. They will know you are more connected to technology and reliable because of that.

The first suggestion for new gadgets to use would be a smart speaker. This is something like:

- Amazon Echo

- Echo Dot

- Google Home Mini

You can sync these with Alexa and have a host in the home to help improve the guest's experience. They can ask Alexa questions about the home, such as what the wifi password is. They can ask her about different locations they could go, such as restaurants or bars in the area. The smart speaker is great for music, and you can have different chargers and electronic accessories so they can use their devices with it as well.

Having a video doorbell can be important. Any home should have protection against potential theft or burglary, and the video use means you can also monitor who is coming in and out of the home. If you have a strict limitation on the number of guests, you can ensure that they are not breaking the rules. You can also use this doorbell to identify if someone needs let in. You can unlock the door from your location for a guest who might have forgotten the passcode or locked their keys inside. These include some like:

- SkyBell

- August Doorbell Cam

A smart thermostat is a great addition as well. This way you can make sure no one is blasting the heat or air too high for extended periods of time. You want to make sure your guests are comfortable, so don't be too stingy all of the time. However, you can make sure that they also turn it off after they've left, especially if there is a gap until the next guests arrive. These include devices like:

- Google Nest Tag

- Ecobee Ecobee3 Lite

- Emerson Sensi

Just like a smart thermostat, a smart light is also a good investment because it can help to make sure that you are managing the lights when others might not be around. These are extra features that can make user experiences better because they can adjust brightness or even color.

Motion sensors are good especially if you want to block off certain parts of the property. Whether you want to block off the basement, attic, garage, or backyard, you can install a motion sensor to make sure guests are adhering to the rules. Of course, you should lock these parts off as it is, but these features make it easier to know whether or not someone is actually listening to the restrictions you gave them.

Finally, security cameras are a good addition, but there are a few things you need to know. First and foremost, NEVER hide a security camera and make sure any that are in common areas are in clear view and you've listed in the descriptions or emails that there will be a security camera. It is not only immoral to secretly record people, but in most areas, it will be illegal.

A security camera is good for outdoor areas and backyards to make sure that you can protect your property from damage or burglaries. It is a way to make the guests feel safer as well, especially when they are going into an area they don't know.

These gadgets will be expensive at first, but they will pay for themselves overtime. You will always be happier to have had them rather than regretful that you didn't.

Chapter 6: How to Scale and Buy More Properties

After you've gotten this process down, you're probably going to want to start to introduce more properties. Start out with a property in an area that you know well. When you live close to it you can be directly there to manage the property. After you have grown your profit and learned the different mistakes that you might have been making you can move on and look for other areas of investment. This begins by making sure that you are very knowledgeable of the different settings that you're going to invest in. If you are not careful, then you can end up causing huge mistakes by investing in the wrong properties.

With all this new money made as a host, you can use that to make even more money with investment properties! There's nothing better than money that makes more money. In this chapter we're going to go over all of the steps that you need to take to make sure that you're selecting the perfect location. This will include doing everything from research in-person to studying different analytics online.

There are a few different apps that you can use, which help provide you a ton of user data. We'll go over the best two in this chapter.

You can also use the analytics that are directly in Airbnb to figure out which areas do well, and which areas aren't really worth your time. Make sure that you do research in all areas. Something might seem like it's a great investment because it doesn't cost that much money, but there could be other negative side effects, such as the location or the weather that is frequently in that general area.

The more research that you do, the more prepared you will be for everything that may come your way as a Airbnb host.

Market research

There are a few different steps to market research that you will want to make sure that you are conducting. The first step is to make sure that you pick an area that works. Obviously, there's no point in investing in a property that's in the middle of nowhere with no other amenities around. You want to get as close to the hip and trendy areas as possible. Pick a place that has walking distance to beaches, restaurants, stores, and things like that.

Of course, this isn't your only option. You can also consider if you don't want a property like this and instead are going to be investing in more remote locations that might be in the middle of nowhere. These could be for adventurous types that like hiking or families that want to get away from the city.

If you're looking for something that's going to have constant tourist traffic, then picking a high populated area is better than picking something that's in the middle of the forest that's far away. If you're looking to create workspaces and family getaways, then something that's a little bit more removed might be better for those who are looking for a very private location.

In addition to this, you also want to make sure that you actually know the area. Just because something is five miles from downtown, that does not mean that it is a great location. It could be a nice property within a not so safe area with a high crime rate. You don't want to invest in something unless you're actually there. It's good to check out your competition and even rent out an Airbnb in the place that you are planning on going. You can see what other competitors are like and you can also get a feel for the area so that you can accommodate your property to the type of people who will be visiting. The next step is to make sure that you are doing your research online.

This means making cross comparison between various apps. You also want to look at the analytics of the other Airbnb offerings which are in this area. By doing this you're making sure that you are thoroughly investigating every aspect of where you might be investing your money.

After this, it's time to conduct research on what the actual profit is going to be. You might be able to buy a property with the money you have now and make several thousand dollars a month by renting it out. However, there might be property tax fees and other payments that need to be made, which will be even greater than the money that you'd be making from Airbnb.

If you're not going to be making enough money, then, even though you have a great property and this great opportunity, what is the point of even doing that? You want to know what all of your expenses are going to be and where all of your profit is going to be coming from. You'll also need to consider things as simple as what furniture you're going to be buying. Is it an area that is easy to move a bunch of new furniture into?

You also want to research the past and the future of the area. The past might be a little rough, and it might have had a crime rate, but you can also look towards the future to see if maybe this is a property you could purchase now, and sit on as the rest of the community grows. You also want to see if this is an up and coming area and if it is going to be growing immensely.

Are your property taxes going to be going up? Is your rent going to be going up? Whatever it might be, you have to make sure that you are investing in something that's going to be the consistent price that you're expecting and not something that's going to provide all these random unknown costs.

Using AirDNA and Mashvisor

It's best that you use multiple sources to determine what the most efficient places are. One of the best apps to compare data analytics is AirDNA. It has enhanced features of analytics that Airbnb doesn't have. Unfortunately, it does cost money so there will be more of an investment with this tool. You will certainly get your money's worth, especially when you are going to be investing in multiple properties. The data that has been collected is tracking over 4,000,000 Airbnb properties and collects the public information that is presented.

When you first log into the app, you will be shown the home screen. You can search for your specific location and you will be presented with a few things right away. These are:

- rental demand

- revenue growth

- seasonality

- regulation

Rental demand means how much people might be traveling towards this area. Revenue growth is how much it has changed over time. Seasonality is going to show the difference between high and low seasons. Regulation is measured more positively with a low score, as a high score means low regulation.

There is also a section that is broken down by pricing. These are future rates, average rates, and ADR (average daily rate) range. It helps in this area because you can see active rentals that are available, and what the nightly charge is individually and on average.

It also helps to show occupancy rate. This is important because if a rental has a high rate but no occupancy, it's not going to be providing you as much profit. You will also have access to information about revenue. Select your top cities and then begin to compare based on similar types of locations. Don't just look at the price point - look at amenities. Your location might be 3 bedrooms but the same prices as a 1 bedroom. Occupancy might be different based on the type of people that will be renting the properties.

Another great tool to use is Mashvisor. This is a platform that helps you judge whether your investments are going to be worth it. What's a little different about this is the features of the search engine. You can search by:

- type of property

- median price

- optimal rental strategy

- cap rate

- and much more

You can search by neighborhood, and the map also provides a heat function to know what the variant values of the location are. This isn't going to be as great of a tool for knowing what your specific lots might be in comparison to the rest of the area. When you combine both tools, you can take a look at the most analytics possible to ensure you're choosing the right area.

When selecting your top cities, pick out 3 personal choices. We're going to look at the most popular locations based on the analytics from both apps.

According to AirDNA, the top 3 cities to stay are:

1. San Francisco ($3,445 monthly)

2. Venice ($3160 monthly)

3. Santa Monica ($3,038 monthly)

While these might be the highest earning, they are also the highest cost to keep up with. Consider a place like Kaliua, which is an average of $2,940 monthly, but costs less for rent. While you might be making less per month, you might also be spending less per month.

According to Mashvisor, the top three cities are:

1. Lansing ($2,674 monthly)

2. Tuscaloosa ($3,274 monthly)

3. Dubuque ($2,984 monthly)

These are different from the other list because they compare the area and what does best compared to the highly populated areas. Compare your locations across more than just these platforms as well. The more research that you do, the more assured you can be your are picking the right location.

Selecting your Top Cities

Comparing the best properties is important. As we already mentioned, you'll want to make sure you pick something that's close to you if you have no idea what you're doing at first. After you've invested, it's still important to have a property manager who is closer to make sure that someone will always be there when things might go wrong. Aside from these factors, there are a few steps to take when considering your top cities:

1. Conduct neighborhood research

2. Look at the market of the area (restaurant/store revenue)

3. Do an investment property analysis

4. Conduct a predictive analysis (where is this property going in the future?)

Some of it will simply be experience. Even if you think you know everything there is to know about a property you might run into issues. Perhaps there is random flooding when it rains. Maybe the neighbors are difficult. Perhaps the driveway is hard to get into. Not everything is predictable, but we need to take the time to ensure we do look at all the information that has been provided to us, even when it's something you have to pay for. It will be worth your money.

Top Trends

It's good to make sure that you are keeping up with trends beyond simply areas. You can take a home that is in a seemingly not-so-great area and have some other charming features. You can purchase a home on a lake and transform it to look like a famous home from a movie. You can create an experience for your location rather than having it be solely based on your area alone.

One trend that's occurring now is the design. Rustic is very in at the moment. These include refurbished pieces of furniture and antique features that provide a charm which can't be found at hotels or other places people stay.

Another trend is that people are creating work spaces. These are areas that entire teams of employees can stay at a time while also having an area that they can work. You can have a place in a very worker populated destination, like Silicon Valley, and create an apartment that people will go to so that they can conduct meetings.

Tiny houses and cottages are popular as well. People want that experience as if they are living in a quaint area.

What's important to remember above all else is that you are creating a space beyond just a hotel. They want to feel like they are getting a unique experience where they stay. It's not just where they will sleep and shower. They want to be able to sleep, play, cook, gather, and socialize. Have interesting features, like swings in the apartment, game tables, weird art, and so on.

To recap, the top 3 popular trends at the moment are:

1. Tiny homes

2. Work and business friendly rentals

3. Rustic design

Pricing Strategy

Pricing is all about mindset. You have to ensure that you are in the right mindset to really know how to properly get the most of your money. Sometimes we see big numbers and we get excited. We think that the higher the cost of rent, the higher we'll be able to make. This isn't always the case. The more that you are making, it could be that it's the more that you are spending.

After you've recognized this reality, make sure that you start to really consider all of your costs. Your nightly cost is going to include:

- rent/mortgage

- utilities (water/electric)

- cable and internet

- parking

- cost of supplies (toilet paper, towels, bedding, etc.)

Once this is added together, divide it by 30. That will be the cost that it takes to cover the basic necessities. Then, you want to calculate your average taxes per year. How much will property taxes be? How much will you have to pay on your income tax? Calculate this percentage and you will know what you have to make to break even daily.

Remember now that you are going to have some vacant nights. Whether the season is slow or someone cancels close to the date, you will lose out on a few nights. From there, start by doubling the price. Compare this to other homes in the area. Is that a fair price? If it's way too high then cut it down to 30 percent on top of the cost to break even. Adjust as needed, but remember that other amenities can warrant a higher price. Are you the only home in the area that has a pool? Are you closer to the train system than anyone else? You can add a little more for these kinds of amenities.

If your place isn't renting, that doesn't mean it's necessarily too high of a price either. Maybe your pictures are bad. Perhaps you have a negative review. If everything is seemingly perfect then try reducing the price. In the beginning you will also want a lowered price compared to everyone else in the area. This way that will be the sole reason you will get chosen and you can start to gain reviews. As you have more experience, you can adjust the prices as needed. Consider discounts for things like booking more nights in a row or group prices for other rental properties that you have in the area.

You will have to make some adjusting, so don't put all your hope towards the first price that you set. Eventually you will know what you need to do to make prices even higher, but always give yourself padding so that you're doing more than just breaking even.

Chapter 7: How to Profit Off of Rental Arbitrage

What can you do about Airbnb if you don't have the money to go and purchase an entire home? One option that you might have is that you will be able to use rental arbitrage. This means that you are able to rent a place long-term and charge more for it to rent it short-term. It sounds like a deal! Why wouldn't all renters do this?

For starters, the renters might not want to invest their time into having to manage different guests and take control of all that comes along with short-term renting. It means more cleaning, more discussing with customers, and a higher risk of short-term problems.

Rental arbitrage would basically be when you rent a property for something like $1,000 a month and charging $60 a night. That would mean making close to $2,000 a month. The downside is that you might not rent it out every night.

It's also important to remember that not all landlords or renters are going to be OK with doing this. It might even be illegal depending on your area. It's a great way to be flexible with your property as well. You might travel a lot but want to make extra money, so you can rent out your home when you're going to be on vacations and such. In this section, we're going to give you tips on how to do this and ensure that you are being safe and legal about it all.

Profiting Without Owning Any Property

Owning property can be a risky investment because it's such a long-term commitment. You have to get approved for a mortgage and then you're locked in for decades at a time. You might live a lifestyle where you enjoy travelling but a high mortgage can make that harder. If you rent various properties, this gives you freedom, but less of a chance for return.

Airbnb can allow you to rent out your space that you are renting. You could potentially make rent in just a couple of weeks by renting out your space, meaning you stay there rent-free the remainder of the time.

What you have to know about rental arbitrage is that your landlord might be entitled to a percentage. It can also be illegal, so you have to check in with them first before you go for this type of business model. Even if your landlord agrees, it might be against Airbnb's policy.

Your practical steps for how to do this are:

1. Check in with policies to ensure that it is legal

2. Set up your place just as you would based on our previous tips and suggestions

3. Come up with your price based on rent

4. Make sure you have a place to stay if you're renting out the entire apartment

Sometimes you can even rent out just a singular room. Perhaps you have a second bedroom that is not being used. Instead of going through the process of finding a long-term roommate, you can rent the room out for 10 nights of the month at $50 a night. That's $500 a month meaning you have a portion of your rent paid without having to worry about sharing your space for 2/3rds of the time.

How Much Will it Cost?

The cost will be the same for basic amenities that we have discussed throughout this book. Aside from this, you will have to consider the cost for renters. If you are moving somewhere new, these will include:

- application fees

- deposits and move-in fees

- background or credit check

- filing an LLC (if you have to)

- fees paid to the landlords

Some of these might not be necessary, and if you've already moved in, you likely already paid these. If you are renting these properties randomly and not living in them yourself, then you will want to make sure you are breaking even after these initial startup costs when determining what to charge per night.

Always check-in with the restrictions and regulations of your area and within your building. You might be able to rent, but it might be at a certain price. You might be able to only share a bedroom, but the landlord might want an extra security deposit or a fee for the cost of sharing the space.

Risks

There are a few risks that you have to consider before going with this. First, consider if this will continue to be legal and allowed. You might sign up for a 2-year lease with plans of having rental arbitrage and your landlord approves. However, you might also discover in a year that the city limits your ability to do this or might charge higher fees. Then you're stuck in a lease but unable to make the rent because you were depending on rental arbitrage.

You also have to be cautious because you will still be responsible for damages. If someone breaks an appliance, damages the walls or floor, and so on, it's going to be in your name so you will still be responsible.

Aside from this, the main risk is that you have to ensure you are doing this legally.

Getting Permission from the Landlord

Never try to just "get away" with this. Your landlord might live across the country, be relaxed, and never really check-in so maybe you could get away with it. However, if you do this long term and they do find out, you could be liable for paying them back for some of that revenue. You might get kicked out and be in more legal trouble than you could have even anticipated.

Always be upfront and honest because when you're playing with money, there's not always a lot of room to take risks. Let's go over a few tips to ask your landlord if this is something you can do. When you're approaching your landlord, send them a letter or an email. You can talk in person as well, but be prepared with a business pitch so you can talk everything out in a clear and concise way. Follow these guidelines:

1. Be confident.

Some landlords might be disconnected and not know what Airbnb is. If you are nervous and tell them all of the risks first, they might be turned off. Propose it just as you would any business model.

2. Refrain from talking money right away.

You can mention that they could get a portion, but explain the benefits first. Let them know that you will be the one dealing with all of the work. You will be communicating with guests and you will be liable for some of the damages (of course the guest will too, but in the case of abandonment or no contact it would still fall back on you).

3. Show that you have a trusting history.

If you have been late on rent, had poor communication, or weren't the greatest renter in any other aspect, you shouldn't expect them to agree right away. You want to establish trust so they know this is legitimate. You can use references from past landlords to let them know you are reliable and going to be around for the time being.

4. Focus on the benefits.

Let them know it's a way that you will ensure your rent is already paid. Tell them there will be less occupancy because you will only have to rent a few nights. Share that they will be able to have a larger portion of rent because you will be paying the rent in full, plus a fee.

5. Do research before you rent.

NEVER rent a place with the intention of participating in rental arbitrage if you aren't sure that they will allow this. That's just a bad investment move. Have it all laid out and be honest with the process before you agree to move in, especially if that is the only reason you are choosing the location.

6. Don't mention Airbnb just yet.

Sometimes the app can have a negative connotation and they might also get the idea of doing this on their own, without you in the equation. Others might have heard bad things about Airbnb or are worried that it is a corporate or illegal process. Use other words and be careful with how you lay things out. You want to be as clear as you can about what this will entail and why it's good for them.

7. Get everything in writing.

This is the most important aspect of all. They might agree, but you have to get it all in writing to protect yourself in the future. You want to protect yourself from any retaliation your landlord might take later on. You want to ensure you are doing it all legally as well to protect yourself, especially if those who work for Airbnb start to inquire.

What if the Landlord Says No?

If the landlord says no, you can try to counteract. You can reapproach the deal with a counteroffer - a higher percentage of the portion you would make. You can also try to offer more amenities. Maybe you offer to do the landscaping. Just because they say "no," the first time doesn't mean you can't try to counteroffer. However, gauge their reaction. If they laugh in your face, of course you probably shouldn't try. Some might just feel skeptical because they aren't fully understanding what this process is. Be clear with the details and let them know that this is something which is going to benefit them.

If they say, "no" again, then let it go. You can't force it and you will have to simply search for another way to make money from Airbnb.

The risks that are involved in this process aren't worth it. You might get evicted which could mean that you lose out on your landlords as a potential for references when seeking out a home later. You might have legal action taken against you which could go on your permanent record. You might even discover that you struggle because you get kicked off of Airbnb and banned for life, not being able to use this app as a way to stay in new places.

Your future is something that you don't want to tamper with too much.

Conclusion

The cost of living today is like a jet taking off from the ground—it is quickly ascending to the sky. Meanwhile, making a living is like hiking a tall and steep slope—it's slow and often painful. If you manage to reach the peak, the rewards are extraordinary. However, climbing to the summit takes too much time and effort. If financial stability is the mountain, not everyone is going to be successful in achieving their short and long-term financial goals.

I started writing this book because I recognize the earning potential of Airbnb. Think of it as one of the tools that will help you overcome the peak and reach financial stability. It will make your climb much easier, although I'm not saying that it will all be butterflies and rainbows after you become a host. You still need to work on it. You still need to try your best. I also believe that passion is necessary to become successful in whatever it is you're doing. So if you're just hosting on Airbnb for the money, you will likely fail. It's like trying to climb Mount Kilimanjaro when you absolutely despise hiking. Why force yourself to do something you don't like?

I wrote this book for people like you who are genuinely interested in welcoming people into their homes and giving them a good time. I wanted to help you start this journey and to make your ascent somewhat simpler. If Airbnb is your tool, I am your climbing instructor. I wanted to teach you how to use this valuable tool at your disposal, so you can maximize its benefits and ensure your success as a mountaineer.

In Chapter 1, we talked about the incredible potential of Airbnb and how successful hosts create their action plan. Before any of these, though, we discussed the history of the company. I wanted to include the story of how Airbnb started so you can see the passion that turned the idea into a $31-billion business. Joe Gebbia, Brian Chesky, and Nate Blecharczyk wouldn't have been successful if they didn't believe in their vision. Because of their hard work and determination, hosts now enjoy financial, social, and personal perks. However, you have to remember that even though hosts earn $924 a month on average, there are several factors that affect actual monthly earnings. These include location, capacity, listing type, amenities, interior design, seasons, price, and reviews. There's no need to get discouraged, though. It is possible to earn more than the average if you create a comprehensive action plan. This includes a check-in checklist, a contingency plan, and a growth plan.

In Chapter 2, we talked about how to prepare your property to increase your chances of success. Your pre-opening strategy consists of three phases: customer, property, and dry run. The first phase involves analyzing your target market and creating a customer avatar. The second phase involves performing housekeeping practices, identifying problems that need to be repaired, designing your property, providing amenities, saging your property to remove bad energy, and keeping inventory. Lastly, the third phase is the dry run, which is a simulation of your actual operations. This will give you an opportunity to identify processes that still need to be improved. Before the dry run, you need to create a questionnaire to hand out to participants after their stay, recruit participants to act as guests, and prepare the property. During the dry run, you need to choose a check in method, give guests the best stay possible, and keep hosting until check out. After the dry run, you need to assess its success by conducting a survey and make necessary adjustments based on the results. Although this whole process can be taxing, it is a necessary step if you want to be fully prepared for actual paying guests.

Chapter 3 focused on creating and optimizing your Airbnb listing. First, we talked about the sign-up process. There are four steps that you need to complete: setting up your account, requesting guest requirements, creating house rules, and setting rates and available dates. I walked you through each step and gave you a comprehensive list of all the types of properties, sleeping arrangements, amenities, and additional spaces that you can include in your listing. I also gave you practical tips on how to compose a catchy title and description that will grab the attention of potential guests and convince them to book your place. You also learned how to take pictures of your space to increase listing views and bookings, improve your search results ranking, and refine your listing when necessary. These tips will give you a competitive advantage once you've published your listing.

In Chapter 4, you learned all about the Superhost status. To earn this title, you need to complete four requirements, i.e. complete a minimum number of nights or stays, have an average rating of at least 4.8 in the past year, have less than one percent of cancellations, and respond within 24 hours to 90% of new messages. These requirements may be a challenge for some hosts, but once you've earned it, you get to enjoy exclusive rewards, benefit from more visibility on search results, and get more bookings that lead to bigger earnings. I also answered some frequently asked questions and debunked a few myths about being a Superhost so you can have accurate information on what you need to do to achieve this status.

Chapter 5 was all about automating the hosting processes so that you can focus on having the best business possible. When you can automate some of the simple things, it means you can put more attention on the complex issues.

Chapter 6 is all about finding the right location. You want to put your money towards investment properties that are going to give you the best profit. Remember to not just go for the biggest price tag. Sometimes you will have to start small and work your way up. Always weigh the risks and don't follow the benefits so blindly. There are a lot of things to consider when purchasing a property aside from just the way that the house looks. Does it have other amenities that are close to the area? Are they things beyond just the features of the home that are worth going to? You should also consider extra features that your area might have that others don't, such as a closed in garage.

In Chapter 7 we helped lay out how you can make money from Airbnb without even having to be a property owner. You can make money as a renter and this can give you flexibility. It's less of a commitment and can even act as a trial period as you continue to grow your profits and learn what mistakes you have to overcome. You can take a home that you already have and rent out just the singular room. You could have the potential of making your month's rent in just a few nights, as long as your landlord is going to be OK with you doing this.

You'll have to start small and work your way up. Once you do get to a consistent basis, you can enable yourself to make passive income with your investments. The more research that you do, the easier it will be for you to know what your best options are.

This is a growing business so it's clear that the benefits are going to grow as well. The world demands a unique place where they can have a one-of-a-kind experience. You can provide this all while making money to help improve the quality of your life.

Don't wait for other opportunities to come into your life. Even if this is something that scares you, it might be the very thing that is going to help you make a ton of money. No matter what you might be struggling with in life, money can usually at least alleviate that. It doesn't solve all of your problem and it isn't the key to happiness. It can improve the quality of your life, though. You can get creative and have a unique space where you are expressing part of your design.

This is just one of many ways that you can make more money without having to take on a full time second job. Who knows, maybe one day this could be something that becomes a full time gig, and eventually a way to make passive income. Explore your creativity, get motivated, and never underestimate your abilities to be an entrepreneur.

References

Aydin, R. (2019, September 20). How 3 Guys Turned Renting Air Mattresses in Their Apartment into a $31 Billion Company, Airbnb. *Business Insider*. Retrieved from https://www.businessinsider.com/

Airbnb. (2018). *Amenities Do Matter: Airbnb Reveals Which Amenities Travelers Value Most*. Retrieved from https://news.airbnb.com/amenities-do-matter-airbnb-reveals-which-amenities-guests-search-for-most/

Airbnb. (n.d.a). *Rent Out Your House, Apartment or Room on Airbnb*. Retrieved from https://www.airbnb.com/host/homes?af=43720035&c=.pi0.p k47641205671_211708211456_c_336280738921&sem_positio n=1t1&sem_target=kwd-336280738921&location_of_interest=&location_physical=101 1165&campaign_id=901340844&gclid=EAIaIQobChMIn5DKp K3P5QIV0BwrCh3wZQ7-EAAYASAAEgKfIPD_BwE

Airbnb. (n.d.b). *Airbnb Superhost Program Details*. Retrieved from https://www.airbnb.com/superhost

Airbnb. (n.d.c). *How Airbnb Protects Hosts*. Retrieved from https://www.airbnb.com/d/safety

Airbnb. (n.d.d). *Airbnb's Host Guarantee*. Retrieved from https://www.airbnb.com/guarantee

Airbnb Help Center. (n.d.a). *What Happens to My Payout If My Guest Cancels?* Retrieved from https://www.airbnb.com/help/article/1335/what-happens-to-my-payout-if-my-guest-cancels

Airbnb Help Center. (n.d.b). *What if I need to Cancel Because of an Emergency or Unavoidable Circumstance?* Retrieved from https://www.airbnb.com/help/article/1320/what-if-i-need-to-cancel-because-of-an-emergency-or-unavoidable-circumstance

Airbnb Newsroom (n.d.). *Fast Facts.* Retrieved from https://news.airbnb.com/fast-facts

Bench, A. (2019). Edmonton Police Looking for Man after Furniture and Electronics Stolen from Damaged Airbnb Property. *Global News.* Retrieved from https://globalnews.ca/

Gebbia, J. (2016, February 16). *How Airbnb Designs for Trust* [Video]. Retrieved from https://www.ted.com/talks/joe_gebbia_how_airbnb_designs_for_trusist/details?language=en#t-8410

Kenton, W. (2019a). *Target Market.* Retrieved from https://www.investopedia.com/terms/t/target-market.asp

Kenton, W. (2019b). *Inventory.* Retrieved from https://www.investopedia.com/terms/i/inventory.asp

Leonhardt, M. (2019). 82% of People Think Airbnb-ing Their Home Is a Good Money-Making Strategy—Here's What You Need to Know. *CNBC Make It.* Retrieved from https://www.cnbc.com/

Locke, T. (2019, September 19). Here's How Much Extra Money Young People Make from Side Hustles. *CNBC Make It.* Retrieved from https://www.cnbc.com/

Meiklejohn-Free, B. & Peters, F. (2015). *The Shamanic Handbook of Sacred Tools and Ceremonies*. New Alresford, Hampshire: John Hunt Publishing.

Moghaddam, J. & Momper, S. (2014). Integrating Spiritual and Western Treatment Modalities in a Native American Substance User Center: Provider Perspectives. *Substance Use & Misuse, 46*(11), 1431-1437. doi: 10.3109/10826084.2011.592441

Rapaport, L. (2018, May 8). Many Airbnb Rentals in U.S. Cities Lack Fire Safety Features. *Reuters*. Retrieved from https://www.reuters.com/

Tweedle, S. & Holmes, A. (2019, September 19). $31 Billion Airbnb Announces Plan to Go Public in 2020. *Business Insider*. Retrieved from https://www.businessinsider.com/

MARKET HACKER

The Smart Entrepreneurs Guide to Investing in Real Estate Wholesaling without Passing the Real Estate Exam, Without Being an Agent and with minimal Marketing Power

Baxter Simon

Table of Contents

Introduction

Real estate is an evergreen niche for those who want to make money. The property market in the United States has created an untold number of millionaires, and everyone from your grandpa to Joe College wants to make it big flipping and dealing real estate properties. The demand amongst investors and buyers for real estate has led to a number of tactics evolving over the years, almost all of them complicated.

Terms like wraparounds, reverse mortgages, short sells, and so on, scare away newbies, and all of this is before you begin to deal with the legalities of the sale. Then there's the biggest barrier: The investment amount. The truth is that not everyone has the money to put a down payment on a property even if you are a speculator. Low investment tactics are subjective. I mean to say that what's low in the stock market, for instance, is nonexistent in the real estate market.

Large mounts, such as $30,000, are considered low, and I suppose this is fair given the relative value of the properties you'll be dealing with. Such amounts create an entry barrier and many motivated people get scared away by this. This is exactly what the existing players want since it means there's less competition for them. After all, keeping it an old boys' network suits them just fine. Well, I'm here to tell you that you can make money in real estate without any upfront money. That's right! Sounds too good to be true, doesn't it?

Let me say this upfront. This book is not going to teach you get rich quick schemes. Even if such things exist, I personally doubt they work over the long run. Either way, my point is that this is going to take a lot of work to put into practice and you're going to have to master a number of things along the way. You'll also find that real estate wholesaling is not for everyone. Odds are most people reading this book haven't even heard of it. You'll soon see why this is a good thing.

The real estate market sees a lot of trends in not just prices but also in the kinds of deals that occur. Market conditions dictate the supply and demand for such creativity I suppose. In a cash-rich market, you're not going to find too many folks clamoring for deals that require low money or no-money-down conditions. Well, America is in a cash crunch these days, no matter what the stock market tells you, and real estate wholesaling is getting more popular by the minute.

The key to taking advantage of any trend is get in while it's hot. Like everything else, wholesaling might become saturated. This is obvious thanks to the profit potential it has as well as the low financial barrier on entry. If you're the sort of person who's willing to work hard and learn the legalities of this method quickly, you'll be able to take full advantage of this niche in real estate.

Before getting into what wholesaling is, let's define what it isn't. It is not flipping houses. You will not be performing repairs on the properties you get access to; although, you can choose to fix them up if you so wish. Second, wholesaling is not fully appreciated in every state in America and the laws differ. You will need to do your homework with regards to legalities and what you can and cannot do. In this regard, I'll walk you through everything you need to know, but this is something you should keep in mind.

Wholesaling is a creative way of making money on a real estate deal, and you'll mostly be a middleman. The truth is that the government hasn't quite figured out how to police this portion of real estate dealing, and a lot is left up to the ethics of parties involved. This does not mean it is illegal in any way whatsoever, so you can be rest assured on that. It's just that you have the opportunity to get creative with your deals, and this is a double-edged sword. When starting out, you'll need to be on the lookout for terms of the deal that have the potential to leave you in a jam. This is why preparation is extremely important.

By the end of this book you will have a good grasp on all the aspects of the wholesaling process. This is when the real work begins. Reading this book once isn't enough; you need to review the material in here over and over until you master it. Then, you need to go out and put all of this into action. Once you start taking action, you'll find that a lot of the wrinkles and tips I mention in this book will make a lot more sense.

Ultimately, your success is in your hands. This is a very good thing. You don't want to be involved in a business that requires the participation of several parties or one that depends on a number of factors outside of your control. Real estate wholesaling is a wonderful way for newbies to enter the market and figure out how they can secure their and their family's financial future.

Like with everything else, wholesaling success depends on the strength of your network and how well you can work with the parties involved in the deal. Keep hammering away until you achieve success; there's just no other way to get there. A lot of the jargon will be intimidating at first, but don't let this scare you away. A good way to think of jargon is to remember that all these words are just fancy names for simple things. They're made up by the existing crowd to keep competition low. So don't let this deter you.

So enough talk! It's time to teach you how you can get rich wholesaling real estate, so let's jump right into it.

Chapter 1:
How to Capitalize?

So what is real estate wholesaling exactly? Wholesaling often conjures images of retail wholesalers where you walk into a large warehouse and buy stuff by the pound for a lesser price. Think Sam's Club or Costco. The fact is that retail wholesaling is an extremely capital intensive task and requires huge man hours to pull off. Real estate wholesaling isn't quite that.

This chapter is going to give you a quick introduction to the entire process and into who can do this. In addition, I'll also talk about how much money you can expect to make and some ground realities of the business.

Retail vs Real Estate

Wholesaling real estate is a pretty straightforward process. You find a motivated seller and hook the property up with a buyer and earn a profit on the seller's price and the price the buyer is willing to pay. So is it like being a real estate agent? After all, isn't the profit spread equivalent to an agent's commission? Well, yes it is, but the legalities of wholesaling make the entire deal very different.

When you approach a seller with the intention to wholesale the property, you will need to pay either escrow fees or an earnest money deposit. The latter is usually a small amount and escrow fees amount to a few hundred dollars, up to a thousand. Your upfront investment is much less as a result. Here's why the process is different from traditional real estate agency work. Once you pay the fees, the property is going to be under contract with you in control of the sale.

This is the most important piece of the deal, and once this happens, you're fully entitled to sell the contract onto a cash buyer who will be the ultimate purchaser of the property. This is the essence of the entire transaction. There are a lot of moving parts to the deal, but overall, that's how it works. Wholesaling thus requires very little upfront investment. You can invest as little as $500 and see a return of $10,000 to $50,000 in profits from a single transaction.

Wholesaling isn't for everyone. Let's face it, with such low barriers to entry, the market is full of people looking to pull off a deal. What's more, sellers often look to pocket the additional cash you earn on the sale of their property. Hence, your sales skills and your ability to find good buyers is essential. The seller must truly feel that they have no chance of finding a good buyer without you, so you must bring significant value addition to the deal. There's no free lunch here.

Let's break this down some more.

Your Seller

The seller is the first party of this deal we'll take a look at. Why would someone want to sell a property? Someone who has a great property that is selling for market prices in a good neighborhood is not the person you want to be chasing. Likely, they have a number of options when it comes to people wanting to buy from them or advertise their property for sale.

These kinds of sellers are also not what we called "motivated." In real estate terms, a motivated seller is someone who can't wait to get rid of their property. This can be due to a number of reasons I'll get into shortly. For now, understand that someone who owns a beautiful property in a great neighborhood is not going to entertain your offers, so don't waste your time looking into such places.

The places you do want to look into are distressed sales. Places that are falling apart and which ideally have the owner living in them. Such people have tried their best to fix the place up but have not had much success. They're hoping that a sale is going to give them some return on their investment, and their primary motivation is to take whatever they can get and move the hell out of there. It's not necessary for your sellers to live in the property. You could also have scenarios where an old property is lying around and the owner doesn't know what to do with it.

In such scenarios, you could offer to come in and take it off their hands quickly. The best way to think about doing this successfully is to spot deal scenarios where you can add genuine value. If you cannot do this in a deal, then you're likely going to be undercut. This means the seller is going to realize that they can do this without you, and you're going to be pushed into a gray area from where the seller can simply elbow you out of the way and negotiate with the buyer themselves. Never underestimate the power of greed in this business.

You will find that a seller who is desperate to make some additional cash will threaten you with lawsuits and might even start harassing you at your workplace in order to scare you into backing off. We wish the world was an ethical place, but these often disappear when dollar signs appear. Either way, look at things from a value-add perspective at all times.

Your Buyer

So who is going to buy this property from you and why would they? I mean, why would the seller not contact the buyer directly and work out a deal. Well, there are many reasons for this. The real estate investors you'll be selling this property to will most be flippers. These people look at acquiring property that needs upgrading and then reselling it at a higher price. Often, you'll find that resellers live in the home for a period of two years before selling it back to the market.

The reason is that the US tax code contains a provision where a person can earn a tax free profit of up to $500,000 (for a married couple) if they resell a home they've fixed up (Esajian, 2019). I'm paraphrasing here and this obviously isn't how the legalese reads, but you can see the benefits. There is no more profitable law in the US tax code. Either way, the buyers you'll be dealing with are pretty savvy, and they know what's going on. I mean you'll need to tell them this upfront.

If you're a beginner, you're likely to get squeezed from both sides of the deal. There's no way to avoid this to be honest. I suggest you take what you can get, reasonably speaking, and keep building your experience. You'll find that as your buyer roll expands, you can dictate your profits with more certainty. So why would a buyer come to you? A common reason is a lack of knowledge.

The most successful wholesalers have a knack for unearthing bargains and unknown situations. If you see an ad for a foreclosure in the paper, you're too late. If you hear about it from someone else in the industry, you're too late. If a real estate agent knows about it, you're too late. Wholesaling is 90% hustle and finding the deals that others don't know about. I'll go over how you can find great deals in a later chapter, but know what it is you're getting into.

You might be a novice, but your counterparties aren't. The seller might be someone who's never done this before, but you can be rest assured that your buyer knows what they're doing.

Another reason buyers will come to you is due to the changing nature of the real estate market. Information is everything and local esoteric changes are not fully captured by the MLS system (I'll explain this later). Agents often have vested interests that run counter to buyers, so they're not fully reliable in a changing market. A wholesaler makes a lot of sense since the buyer knows where they stand at all times.

Who Can Wholesale Real Estate?

You might be having some doubts about the whole deal and this is perfectly normal. The reason for a lot of these doubts is the fact that real estate wholesaling isn't exactly advertised anywhere. Conventional real estate literature focuses almost exclusively on buy and hold, flipping, and house-hacking types of solutions. All of these require investment upfront, which totals at least five figures. There just isn't a lot of exposure with regards to wholesaling.

As a result, there are a lot of myths around the process and a lot of experienced investors have no idea about how the whole thing works. Finding someone who can teach you the process is difficult. There are a large number of books written about dealing with foreclosures and buy-and-hold strategies, but there's very little credible knowledge out there with regards to our subject.

First off, anyone can wholesale real estate. You do not need a license to do this and you don't need a specialized education to pull this off. If you have the ability to perform basic arithmetic, you can wholesale real estate successfully. As I mentioned earlier, this doesn't mean it's going to be easy. You will need some skills in place before you can successfully turn this into a full time living. These skills, in no particular order, of importance are:

1. Sales skills

2. Networking know-how

3. Experience

Aside from the third point, it perfectly possible to acquire the first two qualities. Let's take a look at why these are important.

Sales Skills

There's no getting around it, if you're an introvert who likes to sit back and let other people run the day to day while you collect the money, wholesaling is not for you. You're better off making money elsewhere and then investing in real estate notes, which are a passive income source. Either way, that's a different topic. With regard to wholesaling, you need to have people skills.

This is because the deals you'll need to unearth are not going to be advertised in the open. You certainly are not going to have homeowners walking up to you and gifting you deals.

Traditional foreclosure listings are not going to work for you since it's too late by the time news of the listing appears in the usual ad sections. You're going to have to get creative and pound the pavement to find deals.

I'm going to show you the best ways of doing this. However, none of these ways will work unless you build relationships with people. This is entirely a people business and you'll understand why in the next section. For now, you need to work on your sales skills, and most importantly, you need to come across as a trustworthy person.

If you come across as a used car salesman, people are going to treat you like one. Which is to say they'll hate you and try to cut you out of the deal. What's more, the buyers you'll be dealing with will be experienced. They're not going to let you run away with a huge profit margin and you can bet that they'll have a larger network of support professionals than you. Odds are they'll know your own support group better than you.

Thus, you need to come across as trustworthy and likable. If you have issues with this, I suggest finding an alternative method of making money. As far as wholesaling is concerned, you'll be spending almost your entire time negotiating and working out problems one party has with another. If you want to get into this, you have to enjoy dealing with people and whatever they throw at you.

Networking

Your network determines how successful you'll be. The process of wholesaling starts with you not searching for eligible properties but by making connections with the following groups of people:

- Contractors

- Appraisers and title companies

- Lawyers

- Other real estate professionals

Contractors or handymen are extremely important for your business. You're not going to be fixing anything up since that requires investment, but you do need someone to swing by and give you an idea of how much fixing a place up is going to cost. Remember, your buyer is going to take this into consideration when purchasing the property, so you need to know these figures. Here's where you can understand why your people skills will matter. You're not going to be giving the contractor major business, and yet, you want them to meet you and give you an estimate nonetheless.

Why would they do this unless you do a good job of convincing them that you're a reliable person? This is not an easy thing to do, so hopefully you understand why I'm going on about sales skills. The next important party you'll need to network with is a title company.

A title company will give you the inside scoop on the property, and your relationship should be strong enough for them to give you a quick picture of any outstanding liens or any other issues with the property. You'll be giving them work along the way, so this relationship is easier to establish than with the contractor.

Lawyers are everywhere, and while a lot of real estate investors prefer to leave them out of the negotiation and contract drafting process, it is imperative that you find a lawyer who can advise you about the laws surrounding wholesaling. Remember, that the buyer and seller could turn around and cut you out of a deal. You'll also be threatened with fraud when carrying out a deal by a seller or buyer who isn't interested in working with you. If you end up going to court, you're going to need to have a good lawyer by your side who'll always make sure what you're doing is fully legal and above board.

Try finding a lawyer who is a real estate investor themselves. These people will understand the terms of the deal and your objectives better than someone who knows the law. Lastly, you want to network with real estate agents in the area. Agents will not be able to give you any leads nor will they be willing to participate in a wholesale deal. This is because they prefer to stick to regular contracts and don't deviate from the standard playbook.

This being said, there are a few agents who specialize in wholesale deals, but even these people will not be likely to help you. I mean, they can do the deal for themselves so why would they give it to you for a small commission? While you can't expect leads from these people, it helps to know them and tap into their network of buyers. Besides, it's just good business knowing the people who operate in your industry in your area.

Money

So now we come to the real deal. This is what you really want to know, isn't it? How much money you can make and how much investment is necessary. Well, believe it or not, everything that I've said thus far holds true. There are no exceptions or buts. You will find that an investment of $1,000 will be more than enough. In fact, experienced wholesalers get their investments down to ridiculously low sums of $50 and so on.

Your primary expenses are going to be the earnest money deposit and any escrow charges. You will need to pay your title company and the appraiser. The appraiser will help you figure out what a good value for the home is. You don't want an accurate picture, just a brief estimate.

All of this is done so as to be in sync with what the buyer expects and to get a good idea of what your margin and profit is going to look like. You need to find buyers though, and this is going to cost you. Not necessarily in money, but in terms of time.

More than money, it is the time required that throws off a lot of people and catches them off guard. You see, you'll need to spend a lot of time researching deals and building networks with people who can feed you information. Without this, you're not going to get anywhere. While there's no financial investment involved in this, you'll need to be realistic in terms of how much time you can spend on this.

Full-Time vs Part-Time

Is it possible to successfully execute a wholesale plan while doing it part time? Ideally, you want to hang onto your full-time job before switching to this line of work. Well, it is possible but is it realistic? Not very. The only way you can successfully execute this part-time is if you have someone you trust doing the legwork while you pick up on the weekends.

Those who work in shifts will find it easy to execute and divide their time spent finding deals. Those who work white-collar jobs are unlikely to make this work part-time unless they manage to find someone who can source deals for those who are trustworthy. Understand that despite online proliferation, this is still a door-to-door kind of business.

You can employ some tactics which will make it easy for you to passively collect leads, but you'll still need to follow up on them immediately before someone else swoops in on them. Now, my aim isn't to discourage you but to give you a good picture of what it is going to take to succeed. You can execute this business model remotely, but it is going to take initial legwork for you to put this in place.

It is unrealistic to assume that an appraiser, for example, is going to listen to you over the phone and immediately give you a fair value of the property you're interested in. You cannot expect to negotiate with a buyer or a seller over the phone the first time, especially with a seller. You're going to need to invest time. This is true in pretty much every business you look at.

If a business doesn't need too much money upfront, it will need time investment. This is actually a good time to deal with some common myths about the business. It's better for you to understand them upfront in order to understand what you're getting into.

Myth 1 – Remote Investing

There are a lot of gurus out there who will tell you that wholesale real estate deals can be done in the comfort of a beach. This is grossly untrue. As I said, the idea that you can close a deal without setting foot in a property and without meeting the seller or the buyer in person is laughable. No one will deal with you this way unless you happen to be well known, and even in that case, you're going to exhaust your credit with these people pretty quickly doing things this way.

Myth 2 – Wholesaling is Illegal

This is a big one. Here's how you ought to think of it. Driving a racecar outside of a track is a hugely illegal thing to do. However, if you observe the rules and regulations and drive it in areas where you're supposed to, there's no problem with this. Wholesaling is a practice that has a few critical laws governing it that you must be aware of at all times.

The first is to never approach buyers about a prospective purchase unless you have the property under contract. At all times, you need to make sure the contract between you and the seller is solid and in place. Without this, you're hawking real estate without a license and this going to land you in trouble. Not to mention the fact that no reputable buyer will deal with you.

A lot of beginners wonder how they can go about avoiding buyers who seek to undermine them and contact the seller directly. Well, it's really simple. You do things above board and don't cut corners. Buyers who operate in a shady manner will only work with counterparties who are equally shady. So don't make the mistake of trying to outsmart the system or try to be too clever.

Myth 3 – Cut Out the Realtor

Here's the thing, while realtors might not be your best source of buyer information, depending on the market and your property value, they will bring you interested buyers. Even more importantly, they know the laws and will work the keep moving things forward. This myth is believed by those who feel everyone is out to get them and want to scrimp and scrounge on every little thing. Remember that you just need to do things the right way and you'll make this business a success.

This wraps up our introduction to the wholesaling business. Now, it's time to dive in further and figure out the first step to take when sourcing deals.

Chapter 2:
Finding Your Turf

Before you dive into trying to find sellers and properties which qualify, you need to figure out what your area is going to be. Your area or locality of specialization is crucial when it comes to your success. The key to wholesaling well is to dive deep into an area and unearth great deals. The best wholesalers are those who dominate a small area to the extent that buyers have a hard time finding deals before the wholesaler does.

Achieving this result is a function of hard work and experience. However, it all starts with picking an area that suits you and one that you know well. Think of your area as being your circle of competence. You need to know it backwards, and to do this, there are a number of things you must know like the back of your hand. This chapter is going to help you evaluate a suitable area to begin your real estate wholesaling along with the ins and outs of figuring out how you can get ahead of the competition.

Your Turf

Ideally, you want your area or turf to be close to where you're currently living. I mean, it doesn't make sense to live in New York and try to specialize in Des Moines, Iowa. There are a number of factors you should consider when evaluating an area. The factors I'm going to expand on deal with real estate investment as a whole and not just wholesaling. So even if you find that wholesaling isn't your thing, keep these factors in mind in case you wish to switch to another form of real estate investing.

Briefly, here are the factors you need to be aware of:

- Economic factors

- Quantitative factors

- Regulatory factors

Let's look at them one by one.

Economic Factors

The most important economic factor is the population trend. First, you want to operate in an area that has a high population. A lot of beginners find this off-putting and think that they'd do better in a sparser market. Think New York City versus Edison, NJ, for example. Well, here's the thing. The more people there are in an area, the more property there is likely to be. There are also likely to be more potential tenants and sellers along with buyers.

Hence, despite the competition being understandably higher, your opportunities increase exponentially. You can always outwork the competition, but you can't do much if there's no opportunity in the first place. The thing with a small market is that they tend to be very unstable and difficult to break into. This is because they get saturated very quickly thanks to their size. Speaking of size, if a bigger competitor comes in, you're unlikely to hold your own against them.

However, in a bigger city with larger populations, you can carve out a niche and still make a good living. Don't just look at the total population though. What you want to be looking at is the trend. Is the population increasing or decreasing? Ideally, you want a stable population or an increasing one. You're going to need some luck to find a smaller market that is growing quickly, so don't try to shoot for the stars when trying to find a good neighborhood. Be realistic with your assumptions, and you'll find great places to focus on.

In a large city, you don't need to spread out for more than a few blocks thanks to the highly concentrated nature of the population. A good way to get a handle on this is to simply take an estimate of how many properties there are in the area and look at how well you can cover them. Begin with just one potential building if you can manage just that. Resist the temptation of thinking you need to know every single block inside and out. Tailor your business to yourself and you'll put yourself in the best position to succeed.

After the population trends, you want to take a look at the job trends. This is a very important metric to look at. While population growth often accompanies job growth, you want to take a look at the quality of job growth. Are there more jobs being created for white collar people or is there a shift towards more blue collar work? Neither one is better than the other, apart from personal concerns you might have. This is because a shift creates opportunities. When shifts occur, current owners and tenants encounter issues, and this is where you can add value.

If given a choice between a stable, growing neighborhood and one which is growing but is experiencing a shift in underlying population demographics, always pick the latter. You'll just have more opportunities there. It goes without saying that you should ideally be physically close to that area, so don't make demographic change your only criterion.

As an example of what sort of opportunity you might unearth, let's say an area is undergoing gentrification, which is very common in big cities, especially parts of Brooklyn and Queens and parts of the South Side in Chicago. Existing homeowners, especially the ones living in their property will be looking to cash in and move to someplace cheaper. Not all of them can afford to sell though. This is because any rundown neighborhood is going to have homes that are abandoned or in a state of disrepair. This is where you can step in and find willing buyers to buy the property and bail the homeowner out of their mess.

Yes, you'll have competition, but it is important to accept that you're going to always have competition. Let go of the need to find zero competition enclaves. This way, if you do happen upon one, you'll feel luckier than usual. Expectations are the key to success here.

The final factor to look at is the diversity of the economy. What sort of industries exist in the local market that is attracting all these people here? Is it like Detroit of the '60s where auto companies were the sole drivers of the economy or is it like Orlando, FL, which is heavily diversified thanks to its theme parks as well as local industries? The choice is obvious with this one.

You can't always choose to be in a diverse area of course. If this happens to be the case with you, try to see if you can figure out which way that industry is headed. For example, if you were in Detroit in the '80s, it would have been pretty obvious that the place was circling the drain. Do your best to read industry reports and talk to people in the neighborhood. Additionally, things like living costs and inflation provide great indicators of the trend of a single industry dependent neighborhood.

Quantitative Factors

A lot of the metrics in this section won't pertain to you, but you should still be aware of them. Think of this as a research exercise. You're getting under the skin of the local economy and like any good research analyst, your job is to figure out the nuts and bolts of it. The better your research and planning, the better your chances of success. Who wouldn't agree to undertake this, when seen in such a light?

Despite the economic factors, real estate follows a different cycle. Where does this cycle come from and who influences it? Well, who knows? My view is that it exists, so you might as well get used to it. Someone starting out need not bother themselves with macroeconomic factors when it comes to real estate. Instead adopt a local, on-the-ground approach and you'll be fine.

The first factor that indicates the state of the local market is the price-to-rent ratio or the rental yield. The price-to-rent ratio is calculated by dividing the price of the home by the yearly rental amount. The rental yield is the reciprocal of this value. Generally speaking, in America, the price-to-rent ratio is quoted while international markets use the rental yield formula. (Never underestimate America's tendency to be obstinately different!)

A price-to-rent value anywhere from 16 to 20 is considered a good investment for buy-and-hold investors. This is because these buyers will receive a good return on their investment. You might wonder why cap the ratio at 16 and not all the way to one? Well, this is a piece of counterintuitive thinking. Values in this range indicate it is better to rent than to buy and hence an owner is going to have a larger pool of tenants to choose from, thus increasing the pool of stable tenants (Berger, 2019). If your ratio is too low, you're likely attracting a bunch of deadbeats who can't afford to or don't qualify to buy, thereby increasing your problems.

So what does this mean for you as a wholesaler? Well, not much to be honest. This is not a factor you can control and you should not be too swayed by it. Ultimately, the final value (ARV) of the property is what is going to drive your profit so you should focus on that. It is good to know the values though since you can put yourself in the buyer's shoes and figure out their exit strategy and profit. This will help you price your deal better.

The next factor to look at is vacancy rates and the amount of time properties spend on the market. A healthy market will see a quick uptake of properties and decent demand. There's no set marker for this, but it depends on the population density of the neighborhood and its desirability. For example, an apartment in Central Park West in Manhattan is likely to spend a longer time being listed as opposed to one in Red Hook, Brooklyn. Your local knowledge will help here especially since this is a qualitative factor.

The reason you want to track this is because it gives you an idea of the health of the neighborhood and the market in general. If you see too many listing pouring into the market at once and no one buying, clearly it's a warning sign. Indeed, savvy investors realized this back in 2006 in Florida and

California when people were looking to sell their homes, but there were no buyers (Berger, 2019). This predated the credit crisis by almost two years.

You want to operate in a healthy market so always track this along with the unemployment rate.

Regulatory Factors

Regulation plays an important part in investment decisions. You might find a great deal for a potential buyer but high tax rates and unfavorable zoning laws might mean that the overall return they experience will be low. You should educate yourself on this as much as possible, and the best way to do this is to attend seminars on the topic held by real estate associations and network with agents in the area.

Another regulatory factor you should be aware of is the tenant-landlord agreement laws that are in place. When it comes to wholesaling, you'll be selling to house flippers who will look to rent the place out as soon as it's been fixed up. The landlord environment is something you should take into consideration at all times. If it's just too much of a headache to be a landlord in the area, you need to change your buyer targeting and go after those who speculate in property and are in it for a quick profit. Either way, educate yourself with regards to the regulatory environment in your area you'll be well prepared to take your business forward.

Lastly, while this isn't strictly regulation, you want to be aware of the general quality of life statistics in the area of your choice. Things like demographics, the presence of schools, entertainment options and so on influence buyer decisions and, in turn, affect your exit strategy. Crime is another statistic you want to be on top of.

All of these factors are things you ought to be aware of whether you're wholesaling or not. Jumping into the market without conducting this preliminary homework is simply being foolish and you're setting the odds of success against you. A key part of any real estate business is your ability to generate good comps. Not sure what a comp is? Well, let's look at this now.

All About Comps

No matter what your favorite flavor of real estate investing is, generating accurate comps is a huge part of it. Comp is short for comparables. Well, what's a comparable? The term itself is misleading. The best way to think about it to understand that realtors and appraisers look at these numbers to generate the current value and future value of a property. They do this using historical sales data and the current state of the property. There are a lot of other factors that go into it, but it's not relevant for our purposes.

Given the nature of the real estate business, there is a lot of confusing lingo around comps. Understand that when people talk about pulling, running, looking up, getting, checking, reading, or searching for comps, what they're saying is they're going to look at the historical data to figure out the property's future and current value (Martinez, 2019). There's no special knowledge that's being used here, just a few charts and numbers punched into a calculator.

Most homeowners or property owners will run comps in order to figure out what their property is worth if they're looking to sell it. The problem for you as a wholesaler is the future value comp. Some appraisers tend to take subjective factors into account and will sometimes provide a slightly inflated future value. This can lead to some property owners to aim at unrealistic figures. If this occurs, it can be frustrating since the views of a single person disrupt a good thing for everyone, but don't hesitate to walk away if you encounter this. Truth be told, it's more a question of when and not if.

Comps with regard to future value are also important for you because the all-important ARV is generated from this. ARV stands for After Renovation Value and is the value of the property once it's been spruced up (Martinez, 2019). The idea is that you look at the ARV and figure out if the cost of renovations are worth it. Since you'll be selling mostly to flippers, the ARV is a very important number for you. Ideally, you want to find properties that have a much higher ARV than current value, but don't bet on it.

Instead, look to find sure things and move forward steadily. Do note that ARV is also referred to as After Rehabbed Value, After Repair Value, and After Remodeled Value. Don't get too caught up on the jargon, just keep in mind what the spirit of the ARV is and what it seeks to measure. A good way for you to use the ARV is to get a contractor to estimate the cost of repairs and look at your comps to see if the repairs are worth it. Obviously, you need to do this prior to signing a contract with the seller.

The key to wholesaling success is preparation and hustle. The more you prepare your numbers beforehand, the better your chances of scoring a quick deal whose funds you can use to diversify your business. Comps are at the heart of all real estate. So the question now is, how do you go about generating comps? Do you need real estate agents or appraisers? Well, these two are the best and common sources of doing this.

Thanks to technology, there are many other methods of doing so easily and some of them are even free.

Finding Comps

Finding comps online is pretty easy these days. There are two main sources to do so. The first is the Multiple Listing Service (MLS), and the second is through any easily accessible public website. Let's look at these one by one. The MLS is, simply put, the most powerful tool you can have a real estate wholesaler. There's a catch though: The service isn't free and there is a screening criterion. To access the system, you need to either be a licensed broker or an unlicensed broker's assistant (Martinez, 2019). See what I mean when I said networking comes in handy?

The cost of accessing the system as an unlicensed representative will cost you around $25 per month. If smooth talking didn't go your way, you're not left with too many viable options I'm afraid. One option you can utilize is to convince the broker that you're looking for deals and that you'll cut them in on the proceeds of it. This is usually the approach experienced investors take, and it's unlikely to work for you, but it's worth a shot if you can run your mouth long enough.

A second option you have is to access free public websites that pull their listings directly from MLS, and I'll address this later in this section.

The third option you have is a hit or miss one. Realtors customize their websites on occasion to display full MLS data on their own websites. This is done with an intention to generate leads. Check to see if your local realtor is doing this on their website. If they are, you've hit the jackpot.

If the first and third options don't work out, you have the option to check out the free websites. While their listings are quite comprehensive, they're nowhere near as detailed as the MLS is. You see, the MLS contains over 10-years' worth of real estate data and listing information. In addition to this, it also contains all the information that we spoke about in the previous section. So really, you have tons of data right at your fingertips and it becomes very easy to get an accurate snapshot of things.

While the free websites are a great option, it can be a drag finding all the data you need since you'll have to sift through multiple sources. If you can find a way to invest in access to the MLS via an agent, definitely do it since it'll give you a huge edge in not just wholesaling but any real estate ventures down the road.

Public websites that list data for free include:

- Zillow.com

- Trulia.com

- Redfin.com

- Realtor.com

There are a number of other websites, but these are the main ones. These websites usually pull data from MLS and display them for your area. However, they don't pull all available data, so it is a bit limited. If your area is not covered by MLS, then these sources are fantastic. All of them will show you comparable sales in your area and also limited price history along with time spent on the market.

Pulling Comps

Now that you have all this data, what are you supposed to do with it? How do you search for and refine it and use it for your purposes? Well, let's take this step by step. First, you want to reduce your search using appropriate filters. The ones below will do the trick:

1. Area within a half-mile radius from your property

2. Six-month sales history

3. Properties within 20% tolerance range of your property (either 20% greater size or lesser in size)

4. Similar bed and bath count as your property

Remember that point two means you'll be looking at only sold properties within six months and not all listed properties. This is an important distinction to make since the ones that have sold have hard cash behind them. Using a range in terms of square footage will help you develop a range for sold prices as well. This gives you a fair estimate of what your property's value would look like after renovation. Remember, as a wholesaler, you're going to be dealing with properties that will need some sort of fixing up.

Once this is done, check with your preferred contractor with regards to the cost of any repairs and once you add this to the current property price, you have your gross margin. Now from this number, you need to figure out how much you can make.

Truth be told, once you get good at generating comps, you don't need the services of an appraiser. You'll have data at your fingertips and will be able to negotiate with your buyers confidently. The only way to get good at generating comps is to go ahead and generate them. So constantly take a look at properties in your selected area and learn the dynamics. Real estate can be funny in that a single street will cause a fall in property value of 10% or more. So make sure you understand which side of the tracks you're on at all times and watch out for things like gentrification which can enhance property values massively.

A curious case sometimes arises where no matching properties show up on your search. Well, what do you do then? In this case, expand the area to a 0.75-mile radius and look back over a year's worth of sold property. Play around with the bed and bath count as well to get a rough estimate for how much your property should sell. Keep playing with the system and you'll eventually figure out how to generate good comps.

Of course, if all else fails, you can approach an appraiser or a real estate agent.

Chapter 3:
So You're Selling Your House?

So let's talk about finding sellers. These are the folks who're going to sell you their property, and it is your job to convince them that you're not looking to scam them in any way or fashion. This is a tough thing to do. You see, the real estate market is extremely competitive, and you need to strike before the iron is hot so to speak. This is why it pays to niche down into a very specific neighborhood when wholesaling. This way, you can approach people before the listing hits the market.

I'll mention once again that if a foreclosure or some similar listing has already hit the market, then it's too late for you. Buyers have already found out about it and they have likely dispatched offers already. You won't have any wiggle room or anything to add in this scenario so conserve your time by simply not looking at these listings. Don't ignore them completely but look at them just to get a feel for how things are going. Don't rely on them to generate leads. To do this, you'll need to put in some old fashioned elbow grease. This is a good thing since it gives you an edge in your area; something a national buyer will not be able to tap into.

So let's begin by taking a look at who your seller is going to be and why would they even want to sell to you in the first place.

Selling Situations

The nature of wholesaling is that you're not going to be selling properties at market value to your buyer. You're going to be taking a small cut from the overall profit the buyer is going to realize. I'm mentioning this because you need to understand that the thing that makes you the most profit is the acquisition price. The lower this price is from current market value, the greater your chance of making more money. This is a tough thing to do since you'll be dealing with sellers who are in tough situations.

I have mentioned before that some sellers seek to go behind wholesalers' backs and cut them out by dealing with the buyer directly. This often happens when they're in a truly desperate situation and need all the cash they can get. So if this happens to you, don't take it personally, it's just a bad situation overall. It can be a bit depressing locating eligible properties to wholesale since the situations that produce opportunities are pretty bleak. Here are the most common situations your sellers will be in:

1. Bankruptcy or pending bankruptcy

2. Pending foreclosure

3. Default notice on payment or behind on payments pre-notice

4. Divorce

5. Lost job or financial difficulties

6. Family death

7. Behind on property taxes

8. Probate property/inheriting an unwanted house (that's not so bad!)

9. Underwater mortgage (they owe more than the property is worth)

10. Costly repairs needed and no financial means

11. Looking to stop being a landlord

12. Title issues

13. Damage by water or fire

14. Other legal troubles

15. Miscellaneous issues such as deadlines or something else

Point number eleven is worth looking at a bit more before we proceed further. This is when a person has been a landlord for a long time on their own property and are looking for an easier life. While you can wholesale their property, a better option and one that they're more likely to go for would be for you to construct what's called a master lease around it.

This is where you lease the property for them and then sublease it with their approval to tenants. You agree upon maintenance costs and if you think it's worth it, even a payment plan wherein you can buy the building from them via owner financing. The idea is that you collect the profit from tenants' rental payments and the rent you pay the landlord. You manage the property and raise rents by fixing it up or improve it somehow. Owners who agree to this tend to be older in age and don't have the energy to look after things anymore. Convincing them to retire and enjoy a stable cash flow while you do the work is usually a better sell.

In some cases though, they might go for the wholesale approach if they're looking to get rid of it immediately. If this is the case, research why they're selling it. Any owner who foregoes a master lease option for a direct sell probably has negative reasons for doing so since it just doesn't make sense from a financial perspective. I'm not saying it's always nefarious. Just that you need to research the reasons carefully before pulling the trigger on the deal.

As you can see from the rest of the list, except for one instance, everything else is pretty bleak. You'll need to tiptoe around this situation carefully and your empathic skills will be called to task. This is why I mentioned earlier that if you're not fond of dealing with people or have a blunt or dry personality, this line of business might not be best suited for you.

You might be wondering why a seller would choose to go with you instead of the traditional method of listing with an agent? Well, if you look over the list again, you'll realize that people in this situation are desperate to close a sale. Traditional real estate sales take almost two to three months to complete thanks to the paperwork and the financing needed. If you were to walk in and propose that you will find them a cash buyer immediately, you can imagine the response!

Now that we have an idea of what kinds of situations our sellers might find themselves in, let's look at how you can actually locate them.

Locating Sellers

There are two ways of locating sellers, broadly speaking. There are free methods and there are paid methods. Both as equally effective and the profit you'll clear on a deal is worth the investment. Considering that you'll have around $1,000 to play around with, it's a good idea to invest in paid location techniques. First, let's look at the free methods though.

Free Methods

The first method is the tried and true method for accessing the best deal. This involves **driving around** looking for deals. Take a tour through your target neighborhood and look for the telltale signs of a property in distress. Some things to look for are an uncared for lawn filled with weeds, boarded up windows, broken panes, telephone books hanging around or mail piling up near the door. A general sense of unkemptness is a good sign of a property that is distressed.

These properties tend to be abandoned but you'll be surprised by how many people continue to live in such situations. This is because they're looking to get rid of the property and want a quick way out. Now, chances are that they've already listed their property somewhere, but don't let this bother you. I mean, you need to start somewhere! Get out and knock on the door to see who's home.

If you do find someone inside, let them know that you're an investor looking to pay cash for homes and you were wondering whether they would be interested in cutting a quick deal with you. I'll cover what to say and scripts late in this book. Just remember to approach the whole interaction from a standpoint of delivering value. You're not a freeloader looking to skim some money off the top. You're someone who can give them what they want a lot sooner than the traditional channels.

If nobody's home, knock on the neighbors' doors and see what you can find. Check for things like how long the home has been abandoned and if they know where the owner lives. If they do, great! If the neighbors have no clue, you have some detective work to do. Snap a photo of the property on your phone and save it for later use. Next, head over to NETRonline.com, which will give you your state tax assessor's website and phone number.

What you want to do is contact them to find out who the owner of record is for the property and their tax mailing address. Sometimes, the mailing address will be the same as the vacant property; in which case, you're out of luck. If it isn't, you need to send them a letter advertising your interest. You could do some Googling and try to find a number you can call them at. Whitepages.com is a good resource, but this doesn't always work. Either way, send them a letter and include a photograph of their property in the letter and mention that you're interested in buying it for cash.

The photograph adds credibility to your claim by showing that you went around to their place and found no one there. Often, this approach will result in a lead, and from there, you need to use the methods detailed later in this book to take things forward. Make it a part of your routine to check up on properties in your area. Run, jog, or take a walk around the neighborhood and check in on things.

The next resource for you to use is **online classified ads**. This includes websites like Craigslist, backpage.com, and forsalebyowner.com. Filter all listings made by owners to remove the agents. The idea is to find listing which are classified as "FSBO" or For Sale By Owner. Once you have this information up, call them and make your pitch. Lead with your offer to arrange an all cash offer for their property.

Another way to use online classifieds is to screen for FORBOs. This stands for FOr Rent By Owner. Typically, these people will not be as motivated to sell and you're likely to find people who'll waste your time here, but remember, all you need is one lead. Call them to make your pitch and see where it goes.

A great resource for you is to locate Section 8 landlords. Section 8 refers to housing rent subsidies that are provided by the government to low income families. Often, the landlords of these homes tend to be older in age and are sick of the whole thing. You can expand your area when searching for these kinds of landlords provided you conduct your due diligence on the area as mentioned earlier.

A great website for this is gosection8.com, and you can contact landlords for free on there via phone. If you wish, you can even create a free account and send them a mail request. Call them up and ask them how they feel about being a landlord and whether they'd like the burden lifted. The Section 8 method is one of my favorites because it works not just for finding sellers but you can also find buyers by doing this.

If they decline the offer to sell, ask them if they'd be interested in purchasing wholesale deals to add to their portfolio. Section 8 owners tend to either be legacy owners or investors, so if you can land even a single buy lead, this is a huge win for you!

In-person networking is the next way to generate leads with regards to sellers. Your network and the quality of the relationships you have will determine the amount of money you can make in this business. So as a first step, print out some business cards and start distributing them to whoever you meet. Spare no one! Your co-workers, people you meet in line at checkout aisle in the grocery store, someone you meet in a bar, whatever. Keep passing out your cards and use a professional email address. You can get one for next to nothing from Google. Also, rent a PO box from the post office.

Generally, it's bad to have a PO box as an address, but as long as it doesn't look like one, you won't have any issues. The ones from USPS have a suite number attached to them so this is a major plus. When passing out cards tell people what it is you're doing. Tell them how you can arrange the sale of their home without them bearing any closing costs or hassles, in double quick time for cash. As far as sales pitches go, most homeowners will see the value in that.

Attend any industry conference events and network with the realtors in your area as well. Let them know you're around and what it is you're looking for. Sooner or later, you'll get a few bites. The idea is to not just find a few sellers but to find the really motivated ones. Motivated in a real estate context is code for "willing to be lowballed." They're desperate to sell and need a deal ASAP. Someone who isn't motivated is unlikely to accept a low offer, and this reduces your profit margin drastically. So screen your leads carefully and pick the ones who seem the most likely to go ahead with the deal.

Social Networking is a monumental waste of time, but people spend a lot of time on it so you might as well mine it for leads. There are a lot of Facebook groups when it comes to discussing real estate, and this is a great way to build a network of like-minded individuals. In addition to this, you can search for local homeowner groups. The key is to go about advertising what you're looking for in a discreet manner. Don't barge in and start yelling about how you're going to make it rain if they have a home to sell. Instead, befriend the people on the group and interact with whatever topic it is they're discussing in the group.

Change the banner of your Facebook profile to advertise the fact that you pay cash for houses and that sellers can sidestep closing costs and long drawn out procedures during a sale. Let people come to you. You can make the occasional discreet post but don't overdo it or you'll get banned. Another sneaky way of using Facebook is to join local activity groups. Let's say there's a local taxidermy enthusiast group. Well, interact with this group and engage with them by friending them on the platform.

Post status updates on your wall indicating you're willing to pay cash for homes, and as your network grows, you'll get a few leads. You can even set up a referral program where you'll pay anyone who brings you a lead that results in a deal a finder's fee of $1,000. That should motivate people to bring you some leads.

The MLS system is a great way of sourcing great leads for yourself, but to pull it off, you'll need to work with a realtor. In addition to this, you will also need a Proof of Funds document (POF). I'll discuss the POF in the chapter regarding buyers. For now, understand that every offer of yours needs to have an accompanying POF; otherwise, you're going to be laughed out of the place. The way to screen your MLS leads is as follows. Have your agent submit lowball offers on foreclosures, short sales, bank-owned properties, HUD homes (government owned), and REOs. Spot listings show homes that are designed differently from the rest of the neighborhood.

For example, a two-bedroom home in a neighborhood filled with three beds is going to stick out like a sore thumb and the owner is likely hurting. Have your agent send them an offer along with your POF. When bidding on REOs, make sure to instruct your realtor that there should not be any deed restrictions on the property. This is due to the fact that you cannot turn around and offload the property once the sale is complete.

When it comes to REOs and short sales, banks will require you to close the deal before flipping it onwards. This can pose a problem for you, but this is where transactional lenders come into the picture. These people provide short-term loans and enable you to finance the purchase and then offload the property to your back end cash buyer immediately.

As lucrative as the MLS system can be, don't rely on it entirely. This is simply because everyone else is going to be on it, and it will be hard for you to source great deals. As a beginner, you're not going to have much of an edge or experience in dealing with the kinds of deals you'll find and you might find that the deal moves a lot faster than you think. However, try your best to source deals from this and develop a solid working relationship with a realtor.

Utilizing a **website or blog** is a great way to the exposure buy leads for yourself. These days, everyone has an online presence, and if you think about the flow of leads, a blog is going to likely result in you receiving leads before the property hits the market. The trick is to appear to be an authority on the subject of foreclosures or underwater mortgages and then target the local market using local SEO tactics. You can utilize paid ads as well which I'll cover in the next section.

Keep posting great topics that will interest your seller audience on your blog to keep them engaged. Google loves locally targeted posts, so you'll find that not only will your competition be less, you'll also rank higher in the listings when someone from your area searches for you. Popular topics that might interest your audience are things like the foreclosure process in the area, interviews with realtors about real estate prices, profiles and neighborhood demographics, etc.

Of course, at all points on your website, make it clear that you buy homes for cash, and you'll find that once you start getting a few clicks, people will reach out to you preemptively. This is a wonderful way of sourcing leads and will give you a leg up on the competition that relies solely on elbow grease. Focus entirely on local SEO by researching keywords relevant to your area. For example, "foreclosure process for homes in Bushwick" is an example of a locally targeted long-tail keyword versus "foreclosure process for homes," which is a generic keyword.

Publishing interviews and linking out to reputable local realtors will also help establish your credibility and not only sellers but buyers will be able to discover you and understand what you're about a lot better. You also want to design your website so that it is easy for you to collect emails. This will make it easier for you to send your prospect flyers out and generate more leads.

Co-Wholesaling is another intriguing way for you to make money in this business. This works only if you already have a ready list of buyers so keep that in mind. I'll cover the buyer aspect in detail later. Anyway, assuming you have a ready list of buyers what you need to do is approach other wholesalers and check with them if they're open to co-wholesaling the deal.

To do this legally, what you need to do is sign what is called an option contract with them. This contract gives you the option to buy the property at a certain price. Since the contract now names you as a concerned party, you can remarket this contract to your buyers. Your overall profit is going to be a lot lower this way but you'll save a lot of time and money on finding sellers.

This is also a great way for beginners to increase their network and get some deal experience quickly. You'll be dealing with an experienced wholesaler and things might be intimidating, but by being honest about your experience level, you can close deals faster and improve your cash flow right off the bat. The key is to of course find good buyers. As you can imagine, finding sellers is not as hard as finding the right buyers. This is why wholesalers are willing to let other people in on the deal.

Instead of looking at it as an obstacle, view the lack of good buyers as an opportunity to add value to the process. You can find wholesalers using online classified and search for cash for houses listings in your local area.

This concludes our look at free methods of finding sellers. As you can see, there are many ways of going about this and there's no one perfect method of executing this. Do a little bit of everything and screen your sellers by their motivation level to find the best prospects. Now, let's look at the paid options.

Paid Methods

A lot of beginners mentally resist paid methods, but the fact is that these are an investment into your business. If you cannot afford the spend, then you're probably better off looking at some other ways to grow your money. Paid investment works and you need to think of it in terms of return on investment, not just the dollar amount spent. The first form of paid investment we'll look at is **direct mail marketing.**

This might seem to be an antiquated method of generating leads, but it works extremely well. Using a highly optimized script and mailing list, you can expect conversions between 2-5%. When you consider the profits you'll make per transaction then this method is a win-win. Here's how you go about setting this up. First, you need to figure out who you want to send your targeted postcard to.

The best way to figure out who to send your mail pieces to is to go back to the list of potential sellers highlighted earlier in this chapter. Now, all you need to do is find lists of these people. The first place you want to head over to is listability.com and search for the "high equity non owner occupied" list. These are properties that are almost fully owned by the landlord but are rented out. Usually, landlords in these situations are looking to move beyond their properties, and you could land a great deal by getting in touch with them.

Next, build your mailing lists for probate sales by either heading over to the courthouse and getting them for free or heading over to usprobateleads.com. Inherited properties lists can be found at usleadlist.com and realtytrac.com has leads for pre-foreclosure.

Once your list is built, it's now time to take care of your mailing piece. Usually, a simple postcard will do. I recommend choosing a simple yellow postcard for maximum impact. The text on this card should indicate that you would like to purchase their home for cash and create a win-win situation for them by helping them out. On the other side of the card, continue this message and highlight your expertise.

If you have a blog or a website, then let them know about this and encourage them to contact you at your business number (I'll talk more about this at the end of this chapter). Take some time to design your postcard for maximum impact. You can get free templates from canva.com or simply Google postcard templates and create your own.

The question you might now have is how are you going to send all of these out? I mean, you don't see people lugging a bunch of postcards over to the post office and mailing them do you? This is where click2mail.com comes in handy. Using this website, you can create or upload your postcard design and they'll mail your material for you. Once this is done, you need to sit back and track your leads.

Bandit signs are a guerilla marketing tactic and you've probably seen these come election times. The signs blaring "vote for x" are bandit signs and these are a great way to generate attention for your business. The problem is that most of the locations they're placed in happen to be illegal. If you're placing them on someone's lawn or private property, you'll need their permission before doing so.

Placing it on public property is likely to lead to a city ordinance fine and you want to avoid doing this. Of course, there are guerilla tactics such as placing them in a high traffic area on a

Friday evening and picking them up Sunday night but I don't advise this as a long-term strategy.

It's best to meet with private owners and ordinance officials in your city to discuss the legality of your signage. Once this is done, make sure your signs are designed for optimum performance. This means you need to follow high visibility guidelines. Here are some tips to make this work:

- Identify high traffic locations that have great visibility.

- Keep your message short and to the point. Have your information on there such as your phone number.

- Use yellow signs with a black font or any combination of white and red for the background and the text.

- Have your sign be 18X24 inches in size; not more, not less.

- Track your leads.

If done right, bandit signs will generate a ton of leads for you and you should be tracking all of them. This is true of all leads you generate of course, and I'll address how to do this at the end of this chapter.

The next paid option you have are **PPC ads**. PPCs ads are basically Google ads, and these show up on the top of search results. You can target specific keywords that indicate buyer interest. Things such as "cash for x location houses" and so on are great candidates. Using PPC ads in conjunction with a blog is a great way of driving traffic and generating leads for your business.

The downside is that PPC ads are a complete pain to maintain and given the mountain of data that Google gives you on its backend ads platform, you'll need a specialized degree to handle all of it. No really, there is a special course that Google recommends you take in order to master its ads platform. Then, there's the task of maintaining the ads themselves, which is very time intensive.

It might be worthwhile to simply hire an expert at the process, but this will cost you more. While PPC is a great way of generating leads, make sure you have a budget since the ad campaigns will run up costs for you pretty quickly. Also, there's the fact that Google sometimes deliberately obscures the data it provides in order to get you to spend more on its platform (Jones, 2019). So proceed with caution. If you want to skip this option, feel free to do so.

Lead Tracking

There is a lot of information you want to keep track of and the sheer amount of it will make your head spin. So here's how you should be keeping track of your leads and follow-ups. For starters, you want to track the following information on a spreadsheet at a minimum:

1. Address

2. City

3. State

4. Zip code

5. County

The next thing you keep track of the property type. Here's what you need to record in this regard:

1. Number of bedrooms

2. Bathrooms

3. Rooms

4. Units

5. Type (colonial, etc.)

6. Neighborhood type

7. Acres/size

8. ARV

9. Rehab items

10. Rehab costs

Next, you need to keep track of the comps information.

1. MLS number

2. Street address

3. County

4. List price

5. Sale price

6. Sale date

7. Bathrooms

8. Bedrooms

Finally, you want to have another column that indicates whether you've targeted this property and person as yet. You'll be doing this across multiple spreadsheets, so the best way to handle all of this is to take a hint from the way databases are designed and to have keys that connect a listing to another. What I mean is you'll have one spreadsheet containing owner information. Give this a code of some kind that makes sense to you and create a separate column for it.

Now, you create a different sheet that contains property information and record the relevant information into the columns. Link each property to its owner by giving it the same key as the one you gave the owner in the first spreadsheet. Next, link it to the third spreadsheet which has the MLS information using the same key. This way, you'll have some control over the data.

Track the responses you receive from your mailing efforts by using color codes or a separate column. Use the filters on Excel to quickly create a view of which are your active prospects and which ones have gone cold. All of this is a lot of work, and this is why I recommended that you start slow and dive deep into a particular neighborhood at first. Once you figure out how you can track your data well, you'll be in a good position to expand and include more areas in your list.

You can alternatively use paid software like Silead manager or M5 Automated Marketing Machine to simplify the matter.

These are costly and require investment to the tune of close to $300. There is other software out there which charges you a monthly fee for access and these are also very helpful. My advice is to keep costs low and focus on closing a deal first before investing into the business further. It takes work but you can definitely make a success of it via manual tracking.

Aside from this, there isn't much else when it comes to tracking your selling leads. Remember to always focus on the value you can provide when pitching sellers and keep their situation in mind. This chapter contains a lot of information so make sure you go through it again in order to fully grasp what is being said. The trick is to employ as many methods as possible to generate as many leads as you can.

Chapter 4:
Finding the Diamond in the Rough

Once the leads start pouring in, it's now time to start sifting through the ones which make sense for you to continue with. There are a lot of things you should be aware of when doing this. Things such as estimating the value of the property, rehab costs, end buyer profit, and the ARV and so on. Over and above this, there's the small matter of your commission.

Preparing and following a structured process is the best way of making sure you generate top dollar for all your efforts. In this chapter, I'm going to walk you through all the steps you need to take in order to evaluate the property and make sure you end up offering a price that makes sense to everyone involved.

Initial Contact

Once your promotion methods swing into action, you'll begin to receive calls or emails from people interested in selling their property. At this point, your job is to screen them for optimal use of your time. It might seem a bit ridiculous to you, but there are a lot of people who will contact you and waste your time for no good reason. Such people will usually be very interested in what price you can offer them and will often insist on you offering them a price as soon as possible.

When this happens, simply hang up the phone and move on. No true seller in their right mind is going to insist on a price at such short notice. There is a further screen you must employ and this is to figure out how motivated the seller is. You want people who are truly in a position where they want to get rid of the property. They don't want to wait around for the traditional process. Often, despite a property being in foreclosure or being in a decrepit state, owners will prefer to wait around for the usual 60 – 90-day process to finish for reasons known only to them. You don't want to waste your time chasing these people.

All of this can be done by following a simple three-step process as detailed in the following section.

Screening

If you've been keeping a track of your prospective properties, you should be able to pull up its information fairly quickly. At a minimum, you should have on hand the following information:

1. Property information – beds/baths, address, size, year built.

2. Seller information – name, contact number/email.

3. Initial comp data – collected as described in the previous chapter.

To save time, I recommend carrying out comps on properties only once you have a lead. This will save you a lot of time. Initially, when you're unfamiliar with the comp process, it's a good idea to carry out a few hundred (yes, hundred) to familiarize yourself with your area and similar ones close by. This will give you a good base to build upon.

Now that you have a lead, it's time to pick up the phone and give the seller a call. Before the call begins, understand that you want to figure out a few things. These are:

1. The property's story – who, what, why, etc.

2. Rehab costs estimate.

3. Seller motivation – why, how soon, etc.

The property's story simply refers to the history of the place and is a great way to gather information about it that won't come up via regular negotiation. Getting to know the history of the place will also help you appreciate the seller's motivation and why they want to sell the place. More on this later.

Next, you want to figure out what level of rehab is needed on the place and how much it's going to cost you. Ideally, you want to have a contractor on hand to give you rough estimates but you'd be hard-pressed to find a contractor who's going to travel to your property to help you figure out costs for a job they're not going to take on. So it's a good idea to familiarize yourself with general costs. This is more of an art than a science and a good way to do this is to approach a contractor and get an idea of how they estimate things. You will make mistakes with this number at first so build a margin of safety into your calculations as I'll show you later.

Often the seller themselves would have carried out an estimate but take this with a grain of salt. A good rule of thumb is to increase the value of whatever number the seller throws out by 20%. So if they say $20,000, assume it's going to cost you $24-25000. Why would a seller have this number? Well, remember that you're not the only person who's calling them to find a deal. They might have been through pre-foreclosure or might even be in the process, so they'll be aware of general costs.

Lastly, we have seller motivation, which is the most important piece of information you can research. You want to find out why they're selling the property and what they're going to do with the money. While the latter might seem like it's none of your business, it provides a great insight into why they want to sell in the first place. People have all kinds of things going on in their lives. If a person wants to sell an inherited property to fund their kids' college education, then this is excellent motivation, especially if the kids are seniors in high school. This is just an example.

With this framework in mind, call the seller up and spend some time getting to know them. It is important for you to understand that your job is to figure out if you can add value here. Don't approach this with the intention of seeing how much money you can make since this will warp your judgment. If you cannot add genuine value to the seller's predicament, then you're not going to get a deal. A good seller is highly motivated and wants the convenience of getting rid of the property and getting cash on hand.

A simple way of gauging their urgency is to ask them if you made them an offer right now are they willing to wait for a month to receive it or would they like it within 10 days or so? Obviously you want your seller to answer that they want it as soon as possible. This doesn't mean that you should disqualify someone who says 30 days. It's just that they're not as motivated as the other person. Either way, figure out what their situation is and collect all the information you need.

Review whether you have all the information you need. If you don't, go back and get it. Beginners to wholesaling are often afraid of coming across as novices. Well, if this is your first deal, you will come across as a novice no matter how hard you try, so don't worry about it. Besides, sellers don't really care what your experience level is they just want a good deal. It's far better to ask questions and get your doubts cleared as opposed to pretending you know everything and then screwing up later. Lastly, ask them what they want for the place.

Before continuing, make sure you have established contact with an investor-friendly realtor who can help you out with closing deals and establishing escrow accounts. Once this is in place, you are ready to move forward.

Doing the Math

This is the bit that throws off a lot of beginners. This is understandable since the numbers involved in real estate can be intimidating. Again, following a process is the key to reduce the mental burden on yourself. The first step is to check out whether the seller you spoke to is really the owner of the property or not. You can do this by checking the county tax assessor's website as I mentioned in the previous chapter. Fill out this information in your tracking spreadsheet.

One important thing you must check is to see whether they are the sole owners of the property or not. If they aren't, call them back and ensure that all the interested parties are on board. Get the contact information of other people and confirm with them that they're okay with proceeding. Once that's done, it's time to run the comps and estimate the final rehabbed price.

ARVs

Running a comp is as simple as doing what I described in the previous chapter. Take some time to review what was said there. Remember to follow all the criteria as defined and to follow the steps exactly. If you don't have access to the MLS, or if the property isn't covered by it, head over to Zillow.com and get a Zestimate (that's what Zillow calls its value estimate).

This isn't a final definitive value, but it is a good starting point. If the property happens to be in an area you're unfamiliar with or haven't finished your research on, head over to Google Maps and get a feel for the place as much as possible. Note any freeways, power lines, schools, and such. All of these are things that will affect the value of the property.

So now you have two numbers: One is the price that the seller wants and the other is the estimated final value of the place. The difference is your profit margin. Obviously, this number is going to reduce thanks to buyer discount, closing costs, and rehab costs. Either way, you now have a rough idea of what it's going to take to make some money here.

If the margin is too low, pass on it. Generally speaking, you should aim for a profit for yourself of at least $10,000 on a single deal. Remember this is above all the other costs mentioned previously. So you need some wiggle room between the seller's expected price and the final comp value. This is why wholesaling works best on properties that need some fixing up because the more moving parts there are to the deal (in terms of costs and numbers), the more wiggle room you can squeeze out for yourself in the middle.

Now comes the hard part. You need to carry out a comparative market analysis or CMA. This is where your broker comes into play. At this point, if this is your first deal, you're going to run into a snag. What I'm telling you is that your broker is very likely going to not work with you. Why is this? Well, remember that all brokers have access to the MLS and generating a CMA is pretty easy for them. If you give them the address of the property and they see that there's no money to be made for them in this, or if they see that the deal is unlikely to go through, you're going to get fired as a client or investor.

Choosing a good realtor is crucial for your success. When starting out, choose someone who is hungry for success and is willing to absorb a few mistakes. You can frame it as you and them growing your real estate expertise together. The downside is that the CMA they generate might not be the most accurate report. All of this is my way of telling you that for the first few deals you do, you're better off verifying and understanding how to build a CMA yourself. So here's how you do it.

Sold Data and CMAs

The first step to preparing a good CMA is to collect all information about the property. Presumably, you already have this information. Note any changes that have been made recently and so on. You can get this information from the seller. Next, you want to figure out what the tax situation of the property is. This is as simple as gathering data from either the MLS or the county tax assessor's office. You want to pay special attention to the millage rate (the higher this is, the higher the tax rate) and the assessed value.

You might think the assessed value is an accurate one but usually it isn't, especially in the case of old homes which you'll be dealing with quite a bit. The reason is that local counties don't have the manpower to send people out every year to visit properties and collect accurate values. They estimate the value of the property by adding an appropriate inflation rate and move on. This works well for estimating the values of short-term properties but those which have lasted a long time or are below market rate will be inaccurate.

Having said that, don't expect wildly inaccurate rates. There will be a divergence from your final figure and this number but something like a 100% divergence means you've done something wrong in your calculations. Next, it's time to gather sold data for the property. Sold data refers to the information pertaining to the last time the property was sold or changed hands. This data is very important in figuring out what the current expected price ought to be.

The main data points you want to focus on is the price the property changed hands for and the amount of time it was on the market. In addition to this, pay attention to the property trends since the last time it was sold. If you're dealing with a very old property, then sold data isn't going to give you too much information. Newer neighborhoods will have pertinent data though so keep an eye on this.

Whatever price the sold data reflects, you'll need to adjust to bring that in line with current market trends. For example, if the home changed hands a year ago and the market has declined by 3% since then, you'll need to adjust it accordingly. Sold data also has another component to it which is the listing data. This refers to when the home was put on the market last and whether it sold successfully. If it didn't sell the previous time, have any changes been made since then?

You want to get in touch with the seller and figure out why it didn't sell if you see this in the sold data. This will give you a clue as to whether you can make this a successful investment. The next step is to square the number you get from the sold data and reconcile it with your comps. Don't expect it to agree exactly, but the numbers should be in the ballpark.

All of this helps you figure out what the final listing price ought to be. Remember this is the price that the buyer is going to potentially receive once they place this on the market. With this number in mind, you're now ready to visit the property in person and make an offer.

Visiting and Offering

The main purpose of the property visit is to establish the ballpark range of rehab costs. This is not an easy task for a newbie to complete. Often, even inherited homes have rehab needs and you want to arrive at as accurate a number as possible. Remember, you're not going to be rehabbing the property, but you still need to estimate costs correctly since your buyer is going to have to absorb these into their calculations.

So how does one estimate rehab costs? Well, let's look at this in detail.

Rehab Costs

The first step to estimating rehab costs is to actually know the profile of your buyer. I'll cover this in detail in a later chapter but keep in mind that your buyer is going to have different needs depending on their goal. Every real estate buyer tends to stick to certain tracks. Some are flippers, some fix the property and rent it, while some fix it and then live in the place for a while. Whatever their goal is, the rehab estimate you come up with is going to depend on their goals.

For example, let's say you found a fixer-upper in a college town. If your buyer is a buy-and-hold kind of a person, would this make sense for them? Probably not unless they want to rent it out. In that case, your rehab estimate is going to have to take into account the expected cash flow from the property and reconcile that back to the ARV. All of this sounds like a lot, but in practice, it takes about a minute to figure out.

My point is that you need to understand buyer motivation along with seller motivation. While motivation is a euphemism for urgency in the seller's case, it retains its original meaning when we're talking about buyers. Understand their end goal. Ultimately, the buyer's goal is going to make a difference of 5-10% to your rehab costs. This isn't that big of a number but depending on the property price, it could impact your margin negatively. For example, someone who's looking to rent the college campus property out is not going to be too interested in placing high quality kitchen equipment or flooring beyond the bare minimum.

When visiting the property, take lots of photos. Don't rely on memory alone to remember things. Photos will also help you connect with contractors and help you estimate rehab prices. Along with photos, write down all the problems you see and classify them according to the categories below. Actually, why don't you go ahead and turn these categories into a checklist so that you can examine every portion of the place in an orderly manner (Roberts, 2018)?

1. Roof

2. Gutters

3. Siding

4. Exterior paint

5. Decks

6. Concrete

7. Garage

8. Landscaping

9. Foundations

10. Septic tanks

11. Demo

12. Plumbing

13. Electrical

14. HVAC/ Cooling

15. Framing

16. Insulation

17. Sheetrock

18. Carpentry

19. Interior paint

20. Flooring

21. Cabinets

22. Permits

23. Mold

24. Termites/Pests

25. Other

Now comes the legwork. You need to estimate how much everything is going to cost you. The easiest way is to give Home Depot a call and check the prices they offer. Better yet, take your list and photographs over to a contractor you know and have them give you an estimate. As you become more experienced with the process you'll be able to develop a rough estimate yourself.

Initially, don't rush this process since you'll impact your bottom line. Some beginners get pressured by the seller into making an offer on the spot. Don't fall for this trick. If the seller is doing this, they know you're new at this. Counter their tricks by admitting you're a newbie and that you want to take things step by step. If they mention other offers pouring in, simply say you can't help that and that you'll follow your process no matter what.

Prior to your visit, you can also spend time at the likes of Home Depot or Lowe's to get an idea of what everything costs. The salespeople in these stores tend to be former contractors themselves and they'll give you an idea of what things cost. Even better, they'll be willing to put you in touch with contractors who you can network with.

If worst comes to worst, ask someone to accompany you on the site visit. Obviously, you want someone who is experienced to accompany you, preferably another investor or a contractor. Don't worry if you can't find someone. You can always get back to the seller with the final offer later.

Offer

So now we come to the good stuff! How much should you offer? Use the simple formula below (Roberts, 2018):

Maximum offer = (ARV*(1 - Investor discount%)) - Rehab costs - Closing costs - Your profit

Let's take a look at these one by one. First is the maximum offer price. This is self-explanatory. Next is the ARV, which is the final value you estimated using the CMA and comps analysis. Investor discount is a function of your investor behavior. Real estate investors like to apply a standard discount to the ARV to come up with their own buying price. This is effectively their margin after rehab costs.

Usually, buyers will insist on a 20% discount. This means you'll need to multiply the ARV by 0.8 to arrive at the gross margin price (80% of the ARV is what the investor is willing to pay). Next are your rehab costs, which you've figured out in the previous section. Closing costs are whatever your realtor tells you they will be. You can expect this to be around $1,400-1,500.

This is a negotiable part of the deal. If seller prices are too high and are eating into your margin, you can propose that the seller bear this cost. Alternatively, you can offer to bear it or split it depending on how the math works out. Lastly, we have your profit. Fix this at $10,000 and calculate it. Let's look at an example.

Let's say you find the campus property is worth $150,000. This is the ARV and your buyer usually asks for a discount of 20%. You tour the property and find that rehab work is going to cost around $10,000 and your realtor tells you that closing costs are going to amount to $1,400. So what is your offer?

$$\text{Maximum offer} = (150,000*0.8) - 10,000 - 1,400 - 10,000 = \$98,600$$

This is your starting point when it comes to negotiation, which we'll look at in detail in the next chapter. Remember, there are ways to adjust this. The first is that your rehab estimate might be too high. This is ultimately the buyer's headache, but it is possible to negotiate on the basis of this being lower or higher than expected depending on who you're talking to. Next are the closing costs, which I've already mentioned.

Either way, aim for a profit of $10,000 on the deal no matter what. So you have an offer price in mind and now you need to negotiate with the seller. Let's take a look at how this can play out.

Chapter 5:
Make Me an Offer I Can't Refuse

Negotiating with sellers is going to be a little intimidating for you the first few times you do it. This is because you're going to be dealing with people who are in an emotionally vulnerable place and invariably you're going to offend them over something you have no idea about. The key is to accept that you're not going to have it your way and arm yourself for the worst.

This is not to say you should be pessimistic. Just that by tempering your expectations, you're going to ensure you will set the right level of expectations. Beginners get deterred from wholesaling real estate due to their expectations being set far too high and then having it come crashing down. This chapter is going to walk you through the best practices when it comes to negotiating with sellers. While some of these tips will apply equally to buyers as well, we're still focused on the seller at this point in time.

Prepare

Ensure you are well prepared. Carry your research with you to the meeting and be prepared to backup and defend every single one of your assumptions when arriving at your ARV. It's a good idea to role play with someone close to you and have them try to undermine everything you say. This way you'll be prepared to fend off any attack the seller might use on you.

The most common area the seller will question your assumptions about the comps and the values you've derived from them. This usually happens because sellers are looking at the price at which the Joneses sold their home in the neighborhood three years ago and don't know anything about what happened in the locality over the past six months or over the previous year even.

Given the vulnerable state they're in, this makes them doubly suspicious of any lowball offers. During your initial conversation with them, you would have gathered their expected price. If you find that your bid is extremely different from what they expect, call them up first and explain things to them. Remember to take into account any future events that might be coloring their perception of the price. Things such as infrastructure development affect perception a lot.

Remember, a disagreement over price is common, and no one offers their intended price upfront. If anything, accepting a price as soon as it is offered means someone is screwing up somehow. So don't worry about initial disagreement and expect it fully. As you negotiate, have your data handy. You might even want to consider preparing an easily understandable sheet of data for them to peruse. Preparation also extends to understanding what the seller's situation is.

Understand their motivation and take that into account. Remember you're looking to add value and not simply trying to lowball them and make a large profit. Generally speaking, there is no downside to preparation, so go ahead and collect as much data and try to anticipate everything the seller is going to throw your way. You won't be surprised by a curveball by doing this.

Rehearse

I've mentioned the importance of rehearsal in the previous section, but I'm going to mention it again. Remember, you need to prepare extremely well and rehearsal is an integral part of it. Get together with a friend or someone else you trust and rehearse your pitch. Have them poke holes in it as much as possible. A common tactic that is used in negotiation of any kind is to establish a ballpark price.

As the party that is offering you will be looking to lowball the seller and they'll be looking to ask for a price that is higher than what they really expect. Ask your role playing partner to simulate this and prepare for extreme situations like them getting emotionally upset with you.

Another great way to prepare is to actually call the seller ahead of time and run them through the major points of the deal you're offering. Offer them an estimate price and see if they're close to it. Once they agree roughly, meet them in person and negotiate further.

By calling ahead, you're preempting the possibility of any emotional drama in person. Furthermore, if they're in a tough situation, you might find yourself being swayed to accept a lower price and reduce your own profit from the deal. This sort of thing helps no one. Prepare for alternate scenarios such as proposing that they bear closing costs and so on.

If you find yourself mathematically challenged or are uncomfortable with doing math in your head, carry a calculator with you which you can use to run numbers immediately. Role-play the possibility of them throwing numbers at you if you're uncomfortable with them and prepare a coping strategy. A lot of this might seem like overkill, but it is worth taking the time to prepare for worst-case scenarios.

Assert

Research shows that timid negotiators often think they're being extremely assertive when in fact they aren't (Roberts, 2018). We overestimate the level of assertiveness we present in a negotiation and you should watch out for this as well. If this is your first negotiation you need to remember that you are adding genuine value to the transaction and that you deserve to be paid what your time is worth.

Assertiveness really begins with your idea of your self-worth. I'm not saying you need to strut around as if you're worth a million bucks. It's just that you need to have some level of respect for your own time and the work you've put into the deal. If you think that getting paid five figures for a few hours' worth of work is unethical or that you somehow don't deserve it, you have a problem that is going to sabotage your ability to turn this into a success.

Don't admonish or abuse yourself for this. The thing is that people grow up with weird ideas about money, and if you come from a family that doesn't have much of it, odds are that you have no idea what money really is (Roberts, 2018). This is because research has repeatedly shown that people who come from poor families almost always end up remaining poor.

Why is this? It's simply to do with the beliefs we carry around about yourselves and money inside our heads. A good way to tackle your problem is to ask yourself what the money environment was like when you were growing up. Were your parents extremely tight fisted and did they lead you to believe that money was scarce and that there was none of it to go around? Did your father scream and ask you if you thought money grew on trees every time you asked him for some?

People have weird beliefs about money. Whatever the belief, it always comes down to some form of guilt over accepting it into our lives. We think of ourselves as unworthy, of money as being unworthy, and so on. The truth is that money is a necessary aspect of our lives and without it, nothing would exist. Money isn't good or bad by itself. Instead, it only magnifies what is already there. A person who is insecure without money is going to be doubly insecure with it. Someone who is miserly when poor is going to be even more miserly when rich.

Money by itself does nothing and is simply a resource. Think of it as being like water. You need water to survive and the more water you have around you the more you can use it for things. No one carries guilty feelings about water. Yet, money creates all of these illusions in our heads and we fall for them repeatedly.

So become aware of what sort of limiting beliefs you're telling yourself and work to get rid of them. Above all else, understand that your time is valuable and that you fully deserve all the compensation you're asking for from this deal.

Build Rapport

When meeting the seller for the first time, don't rush into the negotiation. Instead, build rapport with them. Ideally, you should have done this over the phone prior to meeting. By asking them about their family, their kids, their dogs and so on, you get them to trust you. This isn't some psychological trick; it is just the way human beings are designed. We are predisposed to conduct business with those we trust.

Hence, your job is not to present the best deal or even add value, although all of those things are important. Your fundamental reason for being in this negotiation is to convince the seller that you're a trustworthy person and that they're not being screwed over.

If you're an introverted person, a lot of this is going to come across as fake but do it nonetheless. Ask the seller about their lives and their hobbies, sports teams, and so on. Always seek to make them as comfortable as possible with you and don't relentlessly focus on the terms of the deal. Build rapport and you'll find that the seller will give you better terms automatically.

Give, Don't Take

All great negotiation is about figuring out what the other person really wants and then giving it to them. What does your seller really want and can you give it to them? Figuring out all of this is a matter of asking a lot of questions and engaging them in genuine conversation. You don't need to learn about their deepest and darkest secrets but you do need to understand their preferred terms for the deal.

When would they like to ideally close by? What is their living situation? What will they be using the money from the property for? Ask as many questions as you can and approach this with an attitude of you trying to give them the best possible value in the deal, instead of looking at it as trying to make the most amount of money.

There is also the fact that your seller is likely going to be in an emotional place in their lives and will need money for something important. So proceed lightly and always learn from your mistakes.

Broaden Yourself

No matter what I say, your first negotiation is going to be intimidating. You're going to be outside your comfort zone. Understand that this is a very good thing. All growth happens outside your comfort zone. At the beginning of this book, you had no idea what wholesaling real estate was or how you could go about doing it. Contrast it to this point in the book where you know how to find properties as well as screen sellers.

Your comfort zone has expanded. So approach negotiation in the same spirit and always be learning.

Chapter 6:
Beauty Is in the Eye of the Beholder

Thus far we've been looking at the supply side of things. We've been focusing on sellers, their motives, and the properties they have. We've looked at how to figure out the fair values of prices for the property and we've looked at how you can make offers and negotiate. Now, it's time to take a look at the person who's going to be paying you money: the buyer.

The right buyer can transform real estate wholesaling into a rip roaring business for you. Contrary to popular perception, it isn't difficult to find buyers in today's markets. This is because people are currently flush with capital and need a place to invest it. Trust in the stock market is at an all-time low and this has led to people turning to the real estate market as a primary investment option.

All of this means you can make money in the market. Given this situation, your task isn't so much about finding a buyer as much as it is about finding the correct buyer. A good and reliable buyer is going to help you close multiple deals and do so quickly. In wholesaling, the speed with which you can close a deal is crucial. Obviously, you don't want to sacrifice quality research for speed, but you get the idea.

This chapter is all about this wonderfully perfect buyer and will show you how you can go about finding these people. Along the way, we'll also look at some of the documents and processes the ideal buyer will furnish you with so as to make your business a success.

Types of Buyers

Just like we took a look at the kinds of sellers you will be attracting for your wholesaling business, let's take a look at who you should be targeting in terms of buyers. This will save you a lot of time and will enable you to tailor your tactics to appeal to such people. Briefly, here are the two kinds of investors you'll want to attract:

- The fixer and flipper

- The long-term rental investor

Both of these groups of people have different objectives, so let's look at them one by one.

The Flipper

The real estate fixer and flipper is a speculative investor. This means that they're looking at a quick gain and a relatively fast turnaround time with their investment. These investors are extremely price conscious and will drive a hard bargain in terms of discounts. They're also very accustomed to appraising properties and estimating renovation costs.

Ultimately, when you're negotiating with these people, you're ultimately haggling over price. In the beginning, you're likely going to find such people for the most part and as much as I'd love to tell you otherwise, it's going to be a baptism by fire. You'll feel way out of your depth talking to them and your price will likely be beaten down a few points.

When approaching such buyers, you want to adopt the 70% rule to pricing. The 70% rule is actually a formula that rehabbers use to estimate their desired purchase price.

Purchase price = ARV*0.7 - Rehab costs

So if the ARV of a property is $200,000 and rehab costs are $20,000, the purchase price they'll be looking at is $120,000.

So this is the price your buyer is looking to pay. Remember from two chapters ago we learned the formula to figure out how much you should offer the seller? Well, this is pretty much the same formula except we're using a deeper discount here (since it's a rehabber they'll want a 30% discount instead of 20%) and we've removed the profit margin component. The difference between what the sellers gets and what the buyer can offer is your profit. So if you want to make $10,000 on the deal, you need to offer a price that is around $110,000 (using the example above).

The upside of dealing with a property flipper is that you'll have both a motivated seller and a motivated buyer who are looking to close the deal as quickly as possible. Remember that the flipper has to renovate the property and resell it onto the market as soon as possible, so you're likely going to see a quick return on the deal. So as with everything else, there are pros and cons involved.

Long-Term Rental Investors

While the flipper is interested in a quick deal, the long-term rental investor is looking at turning this property into a cash flow machine. Their needs are a little bit different. Remember back in the beginning how you researched the rental trends of the area and so on? Well, you did all this in order to figure out the needs of this breed of investor. While the flipper approaches properties using a 70% or 80% rule to pricing, the rental investor is looking at two things.

First, they're concerned with the 2% rule. The 2% rule states that the rental income from a property needs to be at least 2% of the purchase price. In other words, the property needs to yield 2%. Some markets such as densely populated big cities like New York or Los Angeles have a 1% rule, so it depends on the local market. This applies only to the gross yield on the property. You'll also need to factor in the costs they're going to incur.

To do this, you apply the 50% rule. This is pretty simple. You simply multiply the rent they'll receive per unit from the property (which you can estimate using rentometer.com or Craigslist) and divide it by two. From this number, you subtract any insurance or property taxes they'll need to pay. This is their net yield on the property. If your buyer happens to be using mortgage financing, which is unlikely in wholesaling, then you'll need to subtract that amount from the net number (Berger, 2019).

There's no set scale for what is a good net yield, and different investors and markets have different metrics. Either way, you need to figure out their price using the 2% rule and make sure that the costs aren't exorbitant via the 50% rule. Once this is done, you need to subtract your minimum margin of $10,000 from this price and this is your offer price to the seller.

As a backup, see if it squares with the calculation in the earlier chapter. Go with whichever offer is accepted. While these investors take slightly longer to close a deal, it isn't as if they're going to take an entire year on it. You'll find that you can make a greater profit with these types of investors since they'll also be looking at the cash flow component in their investment.

When talking to such investors, it helps to know the rental market well. You don't have to be an expert, but you do need to come across as someone who has done their homework.

These two categories are not the only type of investor out there, but you'll find most of your leads coming from them. In both cases, do your homework and get up to speed on the state of the market. Most importantly, keep focusing on building your buyers list at all times.

Proof of Funds

Your ideal buyer is someone who is willing to invest quickly and more importantly has the cash to do so. Here's an easy way for you to figure out if the buyer is serious. Ask them for proof of funds document when you bring them a deal. You'll need to time this right because you don't want to be wasting the seller or their agent's time. Here's how you do this.

Before sending an offer to the seller, you need to get in touch with your buyer and ask them for proof of funds. This can be a letter or a current bank statement that shows their ability to complete the transaction. It can even be a screenshot of their online banking system with their name clearly shown along with a copy of their ID. This document is good for 30 days from the date on the statement.

Every offer you send your seller needs to have the proof of funds attached to it. Most sellers will not entertain any requests from you unless you produce this document. Some might even ask for it prior to telling you anything thanks to the large number of joker wholesalers present in the market.

Always have the proof of funds ready with you and build your credibility this way. The proof of funds document also needs to have the contact information of the person who is in charge of the funds in case the agent or the seller needs to validate the information in the document.

You must understand that buyers are not going to simply give you their proof of funds documents without building a relationship with you first. Once you establish contact with your potential buyer, you need to build a relationship and get to know them better. Most importantly, ask them what it is they're looking for and refer them to deals that interest them specifically.

For example, if you have a flipper who is looking for deeply discounted deals, don't send them something that can't work and expect them to adjust their expectations. Rental investors are usually very particular about which zip codes they want property in. If your property doesn't match their requirements, don't call them and ask if they can make an exception. Assume their conditions are set in stone at all times. Once you've built up a good relationship, you can take a little more liberty with them. In the beginning, don't.

Remember that buyers want you to bring them deals. So understand that you have a specific role to play and you're going to be compensated for it. They're the ones taking the majority of the risk, so always respect that and add value to their business at all times.

Let's say you've spotted a great deal, but your investor is unwilling to provide proof of funds. This isn't a major red flag by itself as long as you're certain they aren't a fake. Perhaps they don't trust you fully as yet. After all, the proof of funds document can be used anywhere without their knowledge. You've agreed on a price with the seller verbally and now need to send them an offer and a contract with the proof of funds. So how do you do this without causing further delay?

Well, the best way would be to get in touch with a hard money lender. A hard money lender is someone who loans cash to fund real estate deals. They usually work with flippers and are pretty up to speed in terms of what's going on in the market. A simple Google search in your area will unearth a bunch of them. Get in touch with them and let them know who you are and that you're a wholesaler and a renovator. Ask them if you can use a proof of funds letter from them in order to close a deal. Mention that you have a solid partner, but they're delaying sending the proof of funds at this moment.

As ridiculous as it sounds, you'll find that hard money lenders will be willing to provide you with the necessary document (Berger, 2019). The reason for this is that all real estate investors begin as wholesalers, progress to becoming flippers and then turn into buy-and-hold investors. The hard money lender approach is best suited for a particular type of wholesale deal which I'll explain in the final chapter.

Remember that the POF is valid for just 30 days, so don't be that guy who sends an outdated document. Realtors expect the POF as a matter of course and won't mention it to you specifically. It is up to you to provide this.

So now that we know what an ideal buyer looks like and which document you need to secure from them, let's look at how you can go about finding these people.

Sourcing Buyers

You should approach finding buyers as a list building task. Your task is to keep growing your list and keep adding potential candidates to it at all times. As a wholesaler, most of your time is going to be spent networking to find sellers and buyers. So get used to meeting a lot of people and getting to know your turn inside and out. There are many ways of finding buyers so let's look at them one by one.

Real Estate Investment Clubs

This is by far the best way to find buyers and sellers both. While sellers are going to be less in number, real estate investment clubs attract a special kind of investor: the newbie. This person probably has some equity or cash and are looking for the best ways to invest their money. With the stock market doing who knows what all the time, real estate is a far safer bet for folks who have some change to invest.

Such investors tend to be rental investors. An added benefit of meeting such people is that they're beginners as well and they're just as nervous as you are. If you manage to provide them with a good property on their first purchase, they're likely to remember you favorably for it.

In addition to these people, clubs also attract like-minded people and they're good places to get to know all of those who are in the industry. Professionals such as realtors, attorneys, investors, contractors, title company employees, insurance professionals and property managers will all make an appearance at these things and it pays to get the word out and network with them.

Make sure you print out good quality business cards beforehand and spread the word. Let them know what it is you do and how you can help them. Don't go around telling everyone how daunting things are. Instead, tell them you're a wholesaler and are looking to connect investors with high-quality situations for profit. Some people are going to give you the side-eye at this point.

This is because wholesaling attracts a particular type of person. This person believes that wholesaling is easy and it requires very little money to earn a big return. Spend time on any real estate forum and you'll see the inevitable, "How do I make money with no money down?" type posts. Such people are interested in get rich quick schemes. Wholesaling isn't one as I've mentioned before and you should understand that it takes work and you do need to invest money into it.

It requires comparatively less money to execute, but this doesn't mean it is easy to make money. So don't come across as one of these people. The experienced investors in these clubs will give you better insight into what they look for and will usually be open to working with someone who is genuinely interested in learning the business. The key to making these networking events work for you is to connect with people after the event. Meet them for lunch or for a coffee and interview them.

If you approach this as a newbie who is eager to learn, you'll find that most folks will be willing to help you out and will even cut you some slack when you goof up. As long as you're genuine, you'll find a lot of support.

Bandit Signs

We're back to the bandits again! Bandit signs for investors work the same way as they do for sellers. Instead of placing signs that say you buy homes, place signs that advertise a home for sale "below appraisal." Those two words are crucial and will attract your preferred type of investors to you. Place these signs in neighborhoods that you usually frequent.

A good area to place these signs in are crowded junctions near affluent areas. Most investors tend to be rich people and are usually lawyers, doctors, or in such professions. Place them near high traffic areas to gain some exposure. Don't worry about the signs looking cheap, you'll get calls nonetheless.

The question is what do you do when the investor calls and you don't have any properties on hand. After all, you can't control when these calls come in. Well, a good thing to do is to tell them sincerely that the property that was mentioned was just sold but you'd like to get to know their requirements better in order to help them find good deals in the future.

You'll find that most people will be eager to let you know what they're looking for. This is because it is tough to find great places to invest cash, and this is why wholesaling as a business model works so well.

Classifieds

The good old newspaper classified or online classified ad still works. Just make sure you place an ad in the same place at all times. Once investors get used to seeing your ad in the same spot, you're going to get a few inquiries. You can use the same script as you use with your bandit signs. The thing with bandit signs and classifieds is that you're going to receive inquiries where people are looking to move quickly. So ideally you need to have some deals in play before reaching out to buyers who get in touch with you like this.

In terms of online classified ads, Craigslist is probably your best source. There are two ways of sourcing buyers from this site. The direct approach is to head over to the real estate wanted section and look for the keyword "cash." This is going to bring up a bunch of listings from people offering to pay cash for homes. You're also going to find the occasional wholesaler who is searching for sellers. Either way, it's not as if this is going to waste your time. You will find decently motivated buyers here but do pay attention to how old the posts are.

The second approach to source buyers from Craigslist is to advertise the sale of a house below appraisal. Post your ad and you will get inquiries. Again, wholesalers might get in touch with you, but this is not going to cost you much time so it's worth it. Other keywords to search for are "must sell" and so on.

The only downside to Craigslist is the large number of scammers on there. If you have other great sources of finding buyers, then you can safely ignore this. However, when building your list initially make sure you vet these people thoroughly and talk to them to get a feel for their experience level.

Website

The website you created to attract sellers can be used to attract buyers as well. The strategy is pretty much the same as what was detailed in the chapter on sellers. You need to post great content and capture leads via a form on your website. Another good thing to do to attract buyers is post home listings on your website with relevant information. You can also network with other wholesalers to list their deals and charge a fee for it.

This way your website will receive a massive credibility boost in local search rankings and you will attract more traffic and buy leads. This is also a great way to introduce yourself at networking events since people will become more familiar with you via your website. Attending real estate investment clubs will help you interview people and share expertise amongst others in the field.

All in all, setting up and investing in a website is a great decision. It takes a little longer than the other methods, but once it gets rolling, it pretty much perpetuates itself and you'll find that leads will come to you instead of you searching for them. You need to keep engaging your lists of sellers and buyers so running a regular newsletter is a good way to do this. Highlight properties in there and keep focusing on growing your subscriber list.

You could also run paid ads like you did for sellers, but this is going to have a lower ROI for you. Instead, focus on capturing buy leads via a form on your website, hire a few great writers, and get that content machine rolling!

LinkedIn

While Facebook is great for connecting with sellers, LinkedIn is solely to find buyers. You'll usually find these people if you search for the terms "real estate investor" or "fix and flip" and so on. The key with LinkedIn is to make sure your profile picture looks professional. I suggest investing in a professional photographer and have them take a few headshots of you. Whatever you do, don't post a selfie of yourself. This is your professional resume so treat it as such.

Use keywords throughout your profile that indicate a relationship to real estate. When you're first on LinkedIn focus on connecting with real estate agents. You don't need to worry about sending them specially tailored messages, just send them a request and they'll connect with you. Once you get your connections above 500, which will happen in a couple weeks or so, start targeting potential investors by searching for them or searching for them through the networks of the realtors you've connected with.

Send these people a personalized message describing what you do. Don't pitch them anything, just say that you'd like to connect. Once they connect with you, thank them for connecting and tell them that you'd love to get to know their requirements and also mention your website. If they happen to be particularly experienced, ask them if you could interview them for your website. Everyone likes being praised so they're likely to say yes.

Keep posting regularly, about once a day, on the network and join groups dedicated to wholesaling and the real estate business. Just like in real life, you need to communicate and post regularly on there in order to get people to notice you.

LinkedIn has a great feature in that you can post articles on the network. This is a great way to gain exposure and establish authority.

You can repurpose your blog posts and share them on the network to gain some attention. As much as possible, look to connect with people offline and get to know them better. Take it slow and steady and you'll build a good list of buyers.

Seminars

This might seem a bit daunting to those who are a bit shy but why not go ahead and host your own rental investment seminar in your local area? This is a great way of attracting people interested in investing in rental real estate. What if you don't know anything about rental real estate? Well, simply invite someone to speak at the event. You'll have to pay them something but again, this is a form of advertisement.

Publicizing the event is a lot easier than it seems. You need to target people who are close to retirement or who are in higher income brackets on Facebook. The platform allows you to target people according to income so make use of this. Target using demographic or special events in the filters. In addition to this, you can also use direct mail techniques and classified ads to advertise your event.

Create an informative and helpful presentation and let everyone know the ins and outs of rental property investing. When they come up to you and ask questions or engage with you on your website, let them know of any properties you have on your radar currently.

Courthouse Steps

If you thought bandit signs were guerilla advertising, this is super guerilla. The local courthouse sees a lot of foreclosure action with buyers looking to snap up properties right on the steps during the auction. Hang out at your courthouse and spot buyers. If they're bidding on a property, they're obviously looking for a deal and this is where you can help them. As a bonus tip, get there early and strike up a conversation with them to get to know their needs.

This concludes our detailed look at finding buyers for your wholesale real estate business. Remember to do a little bit of everything and don't rely on just one method of finding people. Maintain a schedule of these events and look to help people out and you'll build a great local network of people who you can trust and rely on to close your deals and pay you quickly.

Chapter 7:
Putting It in Writing

Now that we're done with getting sellers and buyers on board, it's time to take a look at the most intimidating portion of this entire process, the contracts. There are a lot of legalities and technicalities involved in wholesale contracts. The good news is that all of this is going to give you a headache the first couple of times you do it. Once past this stage, you'll find that drafting a contract is a breeze.

During your first deal, you need to get a hold of a real estate attorney who will help you draft a contract. There are a lot of free templates available online and you might be tempted to skip the attorney altogether but ask yourself: Is breaking the law worth saving a few hundred bucks?

Now that that's settled, let's dive into the world of wholesale contracts and how the entire process works. This chapter will also make it clear how you're going to get paid. So let's jump in!

The Process

To understand what the deal is with a wholesale contract, we need to take a step back and look at how you monetize the wholesale business model. There are two ways you can make money on a wholesale deal. Technically, your profit is the difference between what the seller wants and the buyer pays. However, the aim is to get paid legally.

The first way to do this is to carry out what is called a contract assignment. Assignment is one of the most common ways wholesalers make money, and this is what I'll be covering in this chapter. The second method is called the double close, which I'll cover in the next chapter since it deals with the closing process. Understand that one method is not more profitable than another. You can use either method no matter the profit.

The double close requires more paperwork and coordination, so wholesalers typically use it for higher dollar amount deals. Like I said, the assignment method is far more popular since it's pretty straightforward. So what does it mean to "assign" something?

Assignment

In real estate contract assignment concerns the buying party. Any contract that has an assignment clause implies that the buyer listed in the contract can sell the contract to another person and transfer the obligations of that contract to that other person legally. The language of the assignment clause is disarmingly simple. In the contract, next to the buyer's name (your name in this case) will be the word "buyer name and/or assigns;". That's it. Those three words indicate that the contract can be legally assigned.

You can think of contract assignment in another way. What this allows you to do is to sell the rights to purchase the home to someone else. The law stipulates that when a real estate contract is executed between a seller and a buyer, the seller is obligated to deal with them. In return, the buyer has agreed to buy an equitable interest in the home and hold the rights to buy the property. These rights cannot be transferred without the buyer's consent.

What this means is that the seller cannot market the home or execute another deal with a different buyer as long as you hold a valid contract. This is what makes the rights to buy a property extremely valuable, and this is why wholesaling works as a business model. The assignment process does not require the buyer to take possession of the title to the property.

In fact, the assignment process doesn't even show up in the title records. So if you assign the contract to your buyer, the title passes onto them once payment is finalized. You or the wholesaler's name doesn't show up anywhere. This doesn't give you any major advantages, but I'm stating this just to help you understand how the process works.

I don't want to give you the wrong impression here. The language of the contract is extremely important and assignment is not just a matter of having the "and/or assigns" clause in there. There's a lot more to it, and you should get in touch with a real estate attorney who can walk you through all the clauses and possible complications.

Assignment Fee

The assignment fee is the amount that the buyer pays the wholesaler. In other words, this is your profit. So how do you get paid? Well, this is entirely negotiable between you and the buyer. Usually what happens is that the buyer pays the full amount into escrow and the amount is split as specified between you and the seller. The language in the real estate purchase and sale agreement will specify how this will be handled.

An important thing to note here is that the buyer usually pays the wholesaler an earnest money deposit or EMD. This amount is paid to indicate their positive intent to complete the transaction. In case the deal fails, the wholesaler keeps the EMD. This amount is nonrefundable, so it is your minimum profit on the deal. There is no set amount for this since it's usually negotiated between the buyer and the wholesaler. If you have a good relationship with the buyer and know them well, you can ask for something as low as $500.

First time wholesalers should protect themselves more and ask for a larger amount. This amount will be deducted from the assignment fee when the deal closes. All in all, it's a pretty simple process really. There are some misconceptions floating around though, and it's worth taking the time to clear them up.

First off, once again, wholesaling is not illegal. A lot of folks think the process of selling a contract is illegal since it looks as if the wholesaler is selling real estate without a license. The truth is that the two processes are wildly different. A realtor advertises the property in question while the wholesaler is selling a contract, not a property. You might say this is a technicality. Well, my response is that it is a legal technicality so why not take advantage of it. Besides, it isn't as if there's anything unethical going on here.

Speaking of ethics, you should disclose to your seller as soon as you can that you are a wholesaler. They'll be worried that you're a joker at this point, but this is why the POF is such a valuable document. You need to secure this before sending any offer and all of the professionals involved in the process will respect you for it and bring you more deals.

Part of disclosing you're a wholesaler is to disclose to them that the assignment clause exists. Another clause that you want in there is one that absolves you of any obligation with regards to buying the property if the buyer cannot close the deal for whatever reason. An attorney will walk you through the language that needs to be inserted to create this situation.

So now that you know the legalese, let's look at how the process of assignment works from start to finish.

The Process of Wholesaling

Here's how the process works end to end:

1. Find the right property

2. Create a contract

3. Submit the contract

4. Assign the contract

5. Collect your fee

6. Party

That last step is completely optional by the way. There are some technicalities to the process so let's take a closer look at each step.

Find the Property

Hopefully you're familiar with the ins and outs of this step by now. Remember, you need to find properties that have sellers who are highly motivated and want to get rid of their property as quickly as possible for cash. The faster they want to get rid of it, the more you stand to benefit. Use all of the marketing strategies listed in this book and you'll be fine.

Remember to keep searching for properties and develop your network via your website by encouraging other wholesalers to post their listings on your website.

Create a Contract

Once you've figured out what you want to pay and have negotiated terms with the seller, it's time for you to draft and create a contract. There are a number of free templates on the web you can use. Download one of these and take them to a real estate attorney to have them look over it. The great thing about this approach is that you need to do this just once, unless a special situation comes up.

A particular point you must let the attorney to help you out with is to clarify your obligations with regards to contract performance. What this means is that, when you assign the contract, you are relieved from its financial obligations, but in some states you might still be responsible for carrying out its performance. So the seller might have cause to sue you in case the buyer doesn't hold up their end of the deal (Martinez, 2019). Hence, incorporate a suitable get-out-of-jail clause.

Most of the time, you can simply show up with a pen and contract at the negotiation and sign the documents right there to close a deal with a seller. Doing this shows them that you are serious. Make sure you carry the POF along with you to show your commitment.

You will definitely encounter sellers who don't understand what contract assignment means, and you'll have to explain to them the entire process of real estate wholesaling. This can be tricky since people won't sign up for something they don't comprehend. Add to the fact that most people don't know of or misunderstand wholesaling and you have a potentially combustible situation on your hands.

Prepare a script beforehand that you can use to explain how the situation will work and how the contract process works. Explain in as simple language as possible the entire deal with the assignation of contracts. It helps to even have a few articles from law blogs saved which will explain the legalities of the process. Go prepared to handle this scenario and you're unlikely to lose out on a deal.

Also, explain the get-out-of-jail clause to your seller. You shouldn't have any problems with this since no reasonable seller is going to see the benefit of suing you in case the buyer breaches the contract.

Assign the Contract

Assigning the contract is as simple as having your attorney draft an assignment agreement between you and your buyer and signing it. The language of this agreement needs to be drafted once and you're good to go for all other deals after that. You are required by law to inform the seller that you have assigned the contract to another person and you should inform the seller of the identity of this person.

The seller will have the proof of funds document or will have seen it at the very least, so they'll know of this in advance. Either way, inform them of where the process stands. At this point, the contract is passed onto your real estate agent or a realtor of the buyer's choice to move proceedings into escrow. Once the contract is assigned and the escrow account is opened, the buyer will transfer the EMD amount into this account and you will be marked the beneficiary.

All that remains to be done now is for the buyer to transfer the money into the account. Motivated buyers usually take about 10 days to complete this, accounting for weekends. There is the closing paperwork and transfer of the title that needs to be taken care of. All of this will be handled by the realtor. All you do is wait.

Collect Your Fee

Once the deal closes, you collect your fee as initially agreed. The most common method is to be paid via escrow. So you'll receive a check in your name for the assignment fee as initially agreed upon. If the buyer fails to close the deal in the agreed-upon time or backs out, you will receive a check equal to the amount of the EMD paid by the buyer. So either way, you earn something, but ideally, you want the deal to close. The seller, upon successful closing, will receive a check for the amount mentioned in the contract you signed with them. The buyer has the title transferred to their name, and they are now the legal owners of the property.

This is how the entire process unfolds. As you can see there's not much complication to it despite all of the legal jargon that surrounds the process. At every step, you can get the help of a real estate attorney or a realtor. In fact, you should involve these professionals if you encounter a special scenario or if it happens to be your first deal. It's better to be safe than to risk filing incorrect paperwork and find yourself liable or even worse, outside the law.

As simple as this process is, there are some exceptions to how it unfolds. Certain states have esoteric laws that you need to be aware of. There's also the process by which you conduct the wholesaling process, specifically when you approach sellers and market the contract to buyers. You need to understand how this works to protect yourself so let's take a look at some tips as well as some exceptions to the process now.

Legal Tips and Exceptions

The biggest point of legality is to do with proving intent to purchase. Intent is established by providing a proof of funds document. Here's the legal way to do things: You find a seller, negotiate terms in good faith, provide them with a POF document, and sign a contract with them with the assignment clause in there. You then assign the contract to the buyer and wait for the deal to close.

This is the illegal way: You find a seller and do not provide them any POF with your offer. Prior to signing the contract, you bring it to the attention of the buyer. As you can see, there's a fine line between the legal and illegal way of doing things and timing the transaction is everything.

Now, I'm not going to lie, a lot of transactions will spill over into the gray area. You will have situations where you'll have sellers asking you whether you have a buyer on hand or not; otherwise, they're not going to deal with you. Some people choose to go ahead with this sort of deal and some don't. The issue with wholesaling is that there's no practical way for authorities to police things and this leads to a bunch of legal conundrums.

Let's take a step back here and examine the process. You're getting hold of a property from a seller and then marketing the deal to buyers. Most states define the marketing of a property without a license as being illegal. Doing this is going to result in a misdemeanor being filed against you and you'll need to pay a fine for illegal practices. Now here's where the confusion comes in. What exactly are you marketing?

Defenders of wholesaling will argue that they're marketing the assignment of a deal and not the property itself. The other side is going to argue that marketing a deal is the same as marketing a home. What's the difference between the two? Both sides have a point in my opinion. Then, there's the way individual states define real estate brokerage practices.

Every state requires you to have a license in order to act as a broker. But who is a broker? In Ohio, anyone who markets a property is considered to be brokering a deal for the property and requires a license to do so (Turner, 2019). Washington doesn't include marketing explicitly in its definition of brokering. Florida doesn't explicitly mention it but makes it obvious that marketing is included. There's no common language. In this gray area, you have a bunch of people operating illegally.

If you have a deal on hand and if you discreetly contact your buyers without listing the property anywhere else, you're not doing anything illegal. I mean, how on earth is anyone going to police something like that? Also, how is it illegal to talk about a property and its terms? If this were true, then talking about a property with one of your friends or spouse would also be illegal.

Then you have the more common case where you see wholesalers plastering Craigslist and LinkedIn with ads for their deals and putting up pictures for the properties and openly soliciting buyers. This is illegal. When you start operating, you'll find that this is a fine line to skirt.

You might be thinking that lawyers ought to know what's going on, but the thing is that every lawyer is going to have a different take on it. This is because of the marketing issue that I mentioned. It's a very subjective clause. For example, what if you simply listed an ad on Craigslist saying you had a contract you were willing to assign on a three-bedroom home without any pictures of the property. What exactly are you marketing here?

The contract is invalid without the property, but the property isn't being advertised in the post. As I said, it's a gray area. So what should you do? Well, the best way to think of this is to ask yourself, if the local commission comes calling and charges you with a misdemeanor, how comfortable are you proving that your intent was not to market properties but only the deals?

In other words, can you show proof that you never carried out mass advertising of properties you dealt with? Can you prove that you didn't bring a buyer to deal prior to signing a contract? Are you even comfortable dealing with a situation like this? If the answer is no, you have two options.

The first is to get your real estate license. This will solve all of your problems and will give you credibility in the market. A lot of people choose this path. Your other option is to carry out the double close, which I had mentioned earlier. In this method, you buy the property and then resell it immediately. I'll go over this in the next chapter.

If you feel you're comfortable dealing with an inquiry into your practices, don't rush ahead and start dealing. First, visit a few lawyers to understand how harsh your state is when it comes to dealing with wholesalers. For instance, Ohio is famously harsh on the practice. If you're living in that state, you're better off getting your license. Florida and California are two other states which are very strict with this issue. The practices I've outlined in this book all assume you're going to do things legally and ethically. Remember to stay on the right side of the law and do things correctly.

Another practice that people usually do, and which you will get punished for, is advertising houses for sale in order to build a buyers list. What people tend to do is they advertise a property, any random one lifted from an agent's site, and list it on their own website or on Craigslist. Upon seeing this, buyers get in touch with them, and at this point, the wholesaler pulls a switcheroo.

They tell the buyer that the property on hand is sold and that they would like to add them to their buyer's list. Understand this: If you have a license, this practice is fine. It's a tad unethical but acceptable. If you don't have a license, this is straight up illegal and you will get caught. The reason for this is that real estate agents are extremely active when it comes to monitoring their turf, and if they notice you advertising one of their properties, you can bet they'll be reporting you to the local commission.

I mentioned co-wholesaling as an option previously. In this

arrangement, you either bring a seller or a buyer to another wholesaler and split the profits with them. If you attend seminars or events that are conducted by wholesaling gurus, you'll be tempted to get into a partnership with another newbie with the idea being that both of you can cover twice as much ground.

Some bigger wholesalers will even recruit you to find cash buyers since there aren't too many credible ones around while they maintain a listing of properties for sale. Doing this is straight up brokering, and you should not do this if you don't have a license.

The double-close method works because you assume the title for the property before passing it onto the buyer. In other words, the title is the key thing in all of this. As long as you're assuming the title, you'll be fine. A lot of information out there takes this fact, twists it around and presents options that are illegal. For instance, there is a misunderstanding that the minute you sign a sale and purchase agreement with the seller, you're assuming title.

This is not the case. Title gets transferred only once the money arrives. As I mentioned earlier, if you're assigning the contract you're not going to show up anywhere on the title deed. So don't think signing an agreement is going to protect you in any way. You'll also have a lot of investors telling you that assigning a contract is perfectly legal so wholesaling is legal.

Understand that the problem is not with the assignation. The issue is with marketing. People assign contracts all the time. For example, contractors engage in this practice quite a bit. However, contractors are not advertising the property at any point in time. Another loophole that some people exploit is the POF letter.

State laws say that you must show ability to close the deal and complete the purchase when signing an agreement. Some wholesalers think that since they provide a POF with the offer, this counts as purchasing ability and, hence, further assignation is perfectly fine. They're right in thinking this way.

However, the issue is again, how did you procure that POF? How did your investors get to know of this property? Can you defend your method of letting them know if the commission comes knocking? How confident are you in your defense? Some commissions are lenient when it comes to enforcing these laws and some are aggressive. The law is subjective. For example, one commission might see the mere fact that the investor was informed of the property after you signed a purchase agreement as being marketing.

Another might consider it as legal since the agreement was signed and informing the investor was a part of the assignation process. There's no set way of doing things here. This is why I'm repeatedly mentioning that it all comes down to how comfortable you are skirting the lines and dealing with the gray areas. There is no way for me to tell you how to stay out of trouble. It depends entirely on the local situation.

If you think legality with the government is your biggest issue, well, I've got news for you. Let's say you get your license and start wholesaling. You'll find that a lot of rehabbers will balk at working with you. This is purely because of the terrible way in which most wholesalers go about the deal.

To a rehabber or any investor, the most important thing is the title. Without this, they have no investment. What a lot of wholesalers do is create a daisy chain. So one wholesaler assigns it to another and so on. Ultimately, you have a situation where the rehabber doesn't know who the original owner is. All the wholesalers in the middle are doing is removing equity from the deal.

This situation will prompt the buyer to simply put the deal on hold and sacrifice the EMD. Once the contract is canceled, they'll simply approach the seller directly and deal with them. Personally, I don't blame the buyer in this scenario. Remember that you need to add value in any deal you do. If you're playing pass with a deal, you're only removing equity from the deal and are not adding anything of value to the process.

From a buyer's perspective, especially a rehabber, there is a greater level of risk for them in a wholesale deal, so you need to address these pain points. First is the issue of the double close. It's great for you but not so great for the buyer. They need to deal with double the closing costs, which adds to their costs and removes profits.

Next is the issue of due diligence time. Most rehabbers will utilize multiple contractors when it comes to figuring out the rehab costs of a project. This takes time. A wholesale contract proceeds on an accelerated timeline, and this creates the possibility that they'll miss something and lose money. If you're part of a daisy chain, you might as well forget your chances of closing a deal since the buyer won't bother dealing with you once they find out.

As you can see, there are a lot of things you need to consider before getting into this business. A lot of them just come down to learning by experience. There is an unfortunate perception in the industry that wholesalers don't add any value to the deal and simply remove equity from it.

Whatever you do, don't believe the word of people who tell you that wholesaling is completely legal without them explaining to you how they go about doing it. Understand the process, speak to an attorney, and evaluate your appetite for risk.

Chapter 8:
Let's Shake on It!

As mentioned in the previous chapter, there are two ways of closing a deal. The first is an assignment, and the second is the double close. The assignment involves a more traditional closing scenario, which you won't have to bother too much with, and I'll go over what you need to do (which isn't much).

The double close involves a little more coordination and you want to use this in specific scenarios. Lastly, you'll also find that on occasion you will need a hard money loan to cover the closing costs. I'll give you the lowdown on how this works and when you need such a cash infusion.

Closing

So, your seller has agreed to terms, and you've hashed out a great price. Once the sale and purchase contract is signed, you can now take this to your buyer and get them on board. The contract will have a specified closing period, and you'll need to pay an EMD fee to the seller in escrow. To do this, you take the contract over to your realtor and get them to open an escrow account and deposit the EMD, which is usually a few hundred bucks.

Meanwhile, the clock is ticking on your getting your buyer on board. This period is usually 10 days long but if you don't have a ready list of buyers yet, this period is extremely short for you to start building a list. Remember, your buyer needs time to inspect the property as well.

If you've done things right thus far, your buyer should be willing to jump on board and to start the process you sign an assignment agreement with them. The assignment agreement is a one-page document your realtor will help you with and both parties sign. Once this is done, your buyer will inspect the property and will close the deal by paying the purchase amount into escrow.

Your fee, the assignment fee, will be mentioned in the assignment agreement. Your buyer will have to use your closing agent (who will be a part of your investor friendly title company) and will deposit their EMD into escrow. This amount is usually up to $2,500, and this is your minimum profit at this point.

After this, you sit back and let things take their course. You receive your assignment fee once the inspection is complete and title has been transferred. The assignment process is extremely simple and doesn't need too much planning beforehand. The downside is that everyone sees what you're making, and if it is too much, you can bet that the buyer is never going to work with you again.

This is why wholesalers have a used-car-salesman reputation in the industry. If you are making a high amount on the deal and wish to keep your profit a secret, then the double-closing method is ideal for you.

Double Close

The double close is also referred to as an ABC transaction or a back to back or simultaneous close. Before the real estate market crashed in 2006, simultaneous closes were the norm and a lot of closing agents were okay with this. These days though, you'd be hard-pressed to find one who will agree to do this for you. This will be relevant for you shortly.

Meanwhile, let's look at the legs of a double-close transaction. In this, you basically purchase the property from the seller and then resell the property to the buyer. Hence, in double close, your name appears on the title. Truth be told, this is the best way of wholesaling real estate since there are no legal issues with this method, unless you market the property prior to the sale.

Also, the sale and purchase agreement you sign with the seller will not have the assignment clause. Everything else remains the same. You open an escrow account with your closing agent and you secure a time period, usually 10 days, within which you need to inspect the property and close within 30 days.

Once this deal is signed and you've submitted your EMD to the seller, you've set up the A-B leg of the transaction. The seller is A, and you're B. Now, it's time to set up the B-C leg. You're still B, and your end buyer is going to be C. The idea behind a double close is to use the buyer's funds to purchase the property while your profit remains in escrow. Here's how it works.

Once you locate your buyer, you sign a separate sale and purchase agreement (along with the EMD) with them and let them inspect the property. Once this is done, the buyer pays you the remaining purchase price into the B-C escrow account. The closing agent lets the funds from B-C flow into the A-B escrow account (less your profit) and the deal is done. You take possession of the title and immediately hand it over to the buyer, and they become the legal owner of the property. Simple, right? Well, not quite. As you can see, a lot depends on the timing of the deal, and as I said before, most closing agents will not let you simultaneously close on a deal.

Before getting into the nitty gritty of all of that, let's first examine the advantages and disadvantages of this method. While double closing is a great way of keeping your profit amount a secret, the issue is that your costs are greater. The biggest contributor to costs are closing fees. Depending on the state you're in, this could run as much as $5,000.

In an assignment, the end buyer takes care of the closing costs of the deal or you can even get the seller to take care of this. In a double close, it's unrealistic to imagine a seller covering closing costs on the A-B leg since it is traditionally the buyer who does this. Remember, the seller assumes you're the end owner of this property. You can get them to cover part of the costs, but they're unlikely to agree to cover the majority of it.

On the B-C leg, you have the buyer bearing closing costs, which is fine. However, here's where most wholesalers spoil the game for everyone else. They expect the buyer to cover both closes for them since there isn't enough of a profit margin on the deal to begin with. If the A-B leg is eating up $2,000 in closing costs and your margin is a total of $5,000, the wholesaler is netting an amount of just $3,000 on the deal. Not very profitable at all.

To secure this original $5,000 net profit, the wholesalers asks the buyer to cover those costs and adds it to the purchase price.

If you attempt to do this, you can kiss your reputation goodbye. Even if the buyer closes the current deal with you, they're unlikely to ever work with you again.

This brings me to my next point about double closes. You need to pursue this method only if there's enough profit in it. Otherwise, there's no point in doing this. some wholesalers try to execute a deal that has a $10,000 profit potential via a double close. This is a waste of time. You're better off assigning the contract instead and let the deal proceed via a traditional close.

So assuming you have enough margin in the deal to make a double close worth it, you now need to deal with the reality that almost no agent is going to let you close simultaneously on a deal. So what do you do? Well, this is where hard money loans come in handy.

Hard Money and Transactional Funding

The term hard money conjures pictures of loan sharks who are ready to pummel you in case you default on a payment, pinky rings, and track suits. Well, hard money lenders aren't your friends but neither are they anywhere as dangerous or disreputable as you might think.

The fact is that this is a highly regulated industry, and there's nothing unsafe about it. Hard money lenders gained an unsavory reputation due to predatory lending practices where they lent money to investors with an aim of foreclosing on the property. You see, in a hard money loan, the collateral is the property itself. If the investor defaults, the lender picks up the property.

This form of predatory lending existed in the earlier part of the previous decade. The real estate crash took care of almost all the unethical people and only the strongest and smartest have survived. As a result, you're going to find that these people know their business very well and will not risk their reputations just to own a piece of property.

Having said that, their terms are pretty steep. You will usually pay around 15% interest on a loan, and you'll also have to pay fees and deposits. These lenders will charge you an origination fee, called points, plus additional fees (called...wait for it...fees). Usually you'll pay 3+ points plus a 1% fee. A point is just a percentage point. So your total fees will amount to around 4% if this is your first loan.

The lender will utilize either the sale value (on the A-B leg) to determine the loan amount or might even take into account the ARV when determining this. Why would they utilize the ARV when they have nothing to do with it? Well, this would be getting into the vagaries of their world and since this book isn't about transactional funding, I'm going to skip over this. Just make sure you understand the fees involved and the loan amount.

Next, you need to understand the loan to value or LTV. Typically, hard money lenders provide an LTV of around 50-75%. So you'll need to usually fund 25-50% of the transaction yourself. In some cases, you'll find that they will provide you a 100% LTV but the deal will need to close quickly. I'll illustrate how you can do this shortly.

As far as the wholesaling process is concerned, you will need a hard money loan when starting out. So it pays to come to grips with the fees and charges they will levy on you and more importantly, find a reputable hard money lender in your area. They usually show up at investment club meetings so networking is the best way to locate them.

Hard money lenders, as I mentioned previously, do a lot of business with flippers. They also expect your natural progression to be from wholesaler to flipper, so you'll find them ready to work with you if you can close deals well. I had mentioned hard money lenders as being a source of proof of funds documents. Well, you use them in the case of a double close as illustrated below.

Using Hard Money to Double Close

The process by which this works is pretty straightforward. It follows the steps below:

1. You find a property and agree to terms with the seller. The wholesaler uses the lender's proof of funds document to make the offer.

2. You find a buyer and agree to terms with them.

3. Both sets of contracts are submitted to the wholesaler's closing agent and separate escrow accounts are opened for the A-B leg and the B-C leg.

4. The hard money lender is contacted by the wholesaler and is informed of the closing date. Terms of the loan are agreed upon.

5. On closing day, the end buyer wires the money to close the deal's B-C leg.

6. On the same day, the lender wires the money to close the A-B leg.

7. A-B is closed followed by B-C.

8. Whatever is left in the escrow account in B-C is the gross profit. The wholesaler pays the fees and other costs to the lender. What remains is the net profit.

Pretty straightforward process as you can see. If the buyer delays the deal for whatever reason or backs out of it, the wholesaler has a problem. In this case, they'll be out of pocket for the fees. While the buyer will lose their EMD, this might not always be enough to cover fees. So make sure you work the math out prior to entering a double-close deal.

Sometimes, the buyer might request for additional time, in which case you need to let the seller know and see if they agree. Given that they're pretty motivated, the seller usually will agree as long as the deal goes through, even if they won't be pleased with you. Your funding in escrow meanwhile can be extended. It isn't uncommon for hard money lenders to provide loans for 120 days or more. You'll have to start bearing the interest costs of course if the term needs to be extended. Given the potential profit on the deal, this is usually not a problem.

You might be wondering how one qualifies for such a loan? Well, traditional loan applicants need to furnish their credit scores and income proofs and so on. Hard money lenders are more businesslike and are concerned with the deal terms. If you can furnish proof that you have a ready buyer, you'll find that most lenders are more than willing to provide you with funding.

In addition to this, the terms of the loan depend on your experience level, your existing assets and so on. Generally, people who come referred are preferred and considered more trustworthy than someone who called the lender off Google.

All in all, double closing is a very lucrative option for a wholesaler. Just make sure you do the math properly or else you'll find yourself with very little tangible profit left. In most cases, assignment is the preferred method.

When approaching a double close, it's best to look at the property as if you yourself were going to fix it up and flip it. This method requires you to do more homework, but in case you hit a snag and your investor backs out, you still have a backup plan in place and can flip the place for a profit. Consider this your Plan B. Who knows, you might inadvertently become a flipper if a double close wholesale deal goes south.

Conclusion

So do you still want to be a real estate wholesaler? As I said in the beginning, this is no get rich quick scheme. You need to put in the work, and more importantly, you need to approach the entire thing from the standpoint of value. Value is what will endear you to the buyer and will help you forge long-term relationships. Without the presence of value, you'll find yourself being cut out of deals and losing contacts.

It is true that a lot of get rich quick thinkers enter this field. It is equally true that when you first introduce yourself as a wholesaler, you're not going to get the warmest welcome. Here's what I suggest. Instead of jumping into this business head first immediately, take the time to educate yourself. This book is pretty comprehensive, but there's a ton of real life situations and wrinkles you will need to learn. It is impossible for me to list everything out in detail.

For example, how would you handle a situation where a seller demands a high EMD, say $3,500 due to the fact that they've smelled your real estate wholesaling technique from a mile away? If you agree to this, your risk is a lot higher because you'll need the buyer to close for sure. Also, if you don't have this money on hand, how will you fund this? There are a lot of moving parts to this question.

Will you consider a hard money loan and fix up the place yourself? Will you assign it immediately? Well, this depends on the numbers. Can you pull off a double close? Given that the seller knows what you're up to is it even worth it? Are you willing to take a little less profit and have the deal go through? Questions upon questions.

Here's how you educate yourself: You start a blog and write a few informative pieces. Once this is done, reach out to influencers and local real estate personalities and interview them for your blog. Of course, your interview is to help you understand the business as well as build a relationship. Instead of presenting yourself as a wholesaler upfront, sneak into their rolodex by presenting yourself as someone who genuinely wants to learn the business.

Needless to say, you can pull this off only by being genuine. This is not a tactic for you to use so don't think about "faking it till you make it." That won't work here and you'll ruin your reputation. As your profile grows, you can present a deal, and you'll find that people will be willing to help you out with the details and practical questions, such as the ones presented above.

Above all else, remember the legalities of what you're doing and ask yourself how tolerant can you be of the gray areas. If you find that you can stomach a little risk, then go for it. If you find that you'd rather be safer, then get your license. This way you'll have complete peace of mind and you'll be able to execute things better.

Another word of caution: You'll find that this is a tough business. There is a lot of potential, but you'll find that there is no shortage of joker brokers who set up daisy chain deals, and you'll hear through the grapevine of a number of deals that have three or four wholesalers involved. For the sake of your own sanity, ignore such people. They'll present themselves as knowing a lot but will ultimately go nowhere.

The same applies to their knowledge of the legality of wholesaling. You'll either find people telling you it's illegal and unethical or that it's fully legal and that you're doing God's work. The truth is somewhere in between as I've repeatedly highlighted in this book. Finding good buyers is the toughest part of this business, and frankly, this depends on the economic conditions in your area.

The best way to find buyers is to hang around places where people have a lot of money. They'll be looking to park their cash somewhere and earn a return on it. Even if you do things correctly, you're going to encounter buyers suddenly walking out on the deal, buyers who are fake, sellers making unreasonable demands, realtors chewing you out because of some protocol you didn't follow and times where the whole thing will seem completely futile.

You'll wonder whether this thing is worth it or if those people who derisively laugh at you and call you a used car salesman are right after all. You'll wonder if the look you get when sellers find out you're a wholesaler is worth putting up with or whether the sideways glance you get from flippers and investors is deserved. If you want to succeed, you'll need to put up with all of this and keep moving forward.

Success is eminently possible. There are very few other professions where you can earn five figures per transaction. The pot of gold is very real.

So, do you still want to be a real estate wholesaler?

Thank you for reading this far, and I hope you've found this book informative. I wish you the best of luck out there and hope you have a smooth path to success!

References

Berger, R. (2019). 3 Key Ratios to Evaluate Real Estate Investments (#1 is All You Need). [online] The Dough Roller. Available at: https://www.doughroller.net/real-estate-investing/3-key-ratios-evaluate-real-estate-investments/ [Accessed 18 October 2019].

Berger, R. (2019). 3 Key Ratios to Evaluate Real Estate Investments (#1 is All You Need). [online] The Dough Roller. Available at: https://www.doughroller.net/real-estate-investing/3-key-ratios-evaluate-real-estate-investments/ [Accessed 18 October 2019].

Esajian, J. (2019). The Best Tax Benefits Of Real Estate Investing | FortuneBuilders. [online] FortuneBuilders. Available at: https://www.fortunebuilders.com/real-estate-investing-tax-benefits/ [Accessed 18 October 2019].

Jones, R. (2019). Google Keyword Planner's Dirty Secrets Revealed. [online] Moz. Available at: https://moz.com/blog/google-keyword-planner-dirty-secrets [Accessed 18 October 2019].

Martinez, A. (2019). How To Find Real Estate Comps To Determine The House Value. [online] Realestateskills.com. Available at: https://www.realestateskills.com/blog/real-estate-comps [Accessed 18 October 2019].

Roberts, E. (2018). [online] Auction.com. Available at: https://www.auction.com/blog/how-to-properly-estimate-repair-costs-on-a-flip/ [Accessed 18 October 2019].

Turner, B. (2019). Is Real Estate Wholesaling Illegal? (Not If You Follow These Strategies...). [online] Biggerpockets.com. Available at: https://www.biggerpockets.com/blog/2015-03-27-real-estate-wholesaling-illegal [Accessed 18 October 2019].

Printed in Great Britain
by Amazon

36053642R00156